Live & LEARN

Terri H. Robinson

A **WORD**Girls Collective

A **WORD**$Girls$ Collective

Foreword by WordGirls Founder, Kathy Carlton Willis

$Live$ & LEARN

Unexpected Lessons from God's Classroom

3G Books

Contents

A Foreword by Our Founder

Live & Learn features first-person stories about times in the writers' lives when they learned unexpected lessons. WordGirls members have carefully crafted their essays using storytelling to deliver meaningful messages for your inspiration and entertainment. The expression *live and learn* has been passed down through time to mean we often learn best in life by experience. Some of us catch on the hard way or take multiple times to learn our lessons. Often when we say, "Well, live and learn!" we mean something in life surprised us and caught us off guard. Lessons come in unexpected ways. There's no book learning (other than the Bible, of course!) for what God teaches us through life experience.

As I compiled the stories from WordGirls, I realized they involved different types of classrooms in life. You'll find the following as you read along:

- Childhood lessons learned
- Hilarious ahas! with ha-has
- Embarrassment as a teacher
- Lessons that helped us do life better
- Mean lessons delivered kind change
- Turning points in life
- Stranger-than-life teachers

Some of our stories have a powerful spiritual lesson, finding God center stage in the vignette. Other stories have more subtle signs of God at work through real-life situations. Sometimes the lesson was a doozy, and other times it could have gone unnoticed if the student hadn't been on the lookout for it. We've learned that even seemingly small lessons can make a big impact when we pay attention. God uses big and small circumstances to help us have monumental moments to carry with us for the rest of our time on earth.

You will find these essays to be a balance of funny and serious, dialogue and narration, weighty and light. Feel free to read straight through or pick out a chapter that suits your day. Our prayer is that *Live & Learn* will help you have your own studies in God's classroom. Be on the lookout. It just might happen when you least expect it!

Your WordGirlfriend,
Kathy Carlton Willis, WordGirls Founder
God's Grin Gal

About WordGirls

In 2014 I had a brainchild to start a group to coach fun, faith-filled women who were serious about the writing life. I served on faculty at national writer's conferences and realized attendees remained stuck in the writing process. I'd see them return year after year with their projects showing little progress. They were often overwhelmed by the conference material and didn't know how to apply it to their writing lives. They needed a group to keep them accountable and a coach to help them figure out their next steps.

WordGirls is a special sisterhood of writing support for women who write from a biblical worldview (whether for the faith market or general market). We propel writers to the next level—regardless of where they are today.

Here's an overview of our exclusive WordGirls benefits:

1. Once-per-year, one-hour phone coaching to personalize your advancement as a writer and/or speaker.
2. Private Facebook group to interact, brainstorm, pray for each other, share ideas, ask questions, etc.
3. Monthly topics to help you grow as a writer. To enhance your learning, the topics will be covered through Facebook group discussions and Zoom live sessions (recorded for you to watch later if you can't make it live).
4. Downloadable PDFs offer extra training in the form of tutorials.

5. Weekly study hall. We designate a two-hour period to work on projects we call our B.I.C. time (butt in chair). Study hall provides added accountability.
6. Periodic challenges. Some challenges are month-long, and others last a season. These challenges will stretch you without overwhelming you. They are guaranteed to increase productivity if you participate. (Participation is not required to be a member.)
7. Digital membership badge to post on your website or social media page.
8. Reduced rates for events and for-fee materials. We have online retreats and WordGirls@Home intensives. We offer WordGirls Getaways as circumstances allow.
9. Opportunity to submit writing for our WordGirls publications.
10. Additional services when you hire our coach for a reduced hourly rate.

To keep the group intimate, we grant a limited number of memberships. We only have open enrollment twice per year: in January (for a February to January membership period) and in July (for an August to July membership period). You'll find a registration form at kathycarltonwillis.com/wordgirls. If you have questions, email kathy@kathycarltonwillis.com.

We also open up the online and in-person retreats to non-members, so keep an eye on the website for details of upcoming events.

Unexpected Lessons

Is Honesty the Best Policy?

by Beth Kirkpatrick

*I*S HONESTY ALWAYS the best policy? When I was growing up, my parents always encouraged me to be honest. I was scrupulous in reporting my younger sister's misdeeds when we were little. However, as I grew older, being honest became more of a challenge. Though I rarely, if ever, told my parents a bald-faced lie, I have to admit there were times when I might have danced around the truth. But imagine my surprise when I caught my dad engaged in a deception of his own!

A Bucket of Trouble

My parents owned a cabin on the Canadian side of Namakan Lake in northern Minnesota in my teenage years. It was a beautiful spot, accessible only by boat. Our water came from the pristine lake and was pumped into the house through the power of a mostly reliable gas-fueled generator. Occasionally, though, there was a problem with the generator. Until it was repaired, we had to haul water to the cabin at the top of the hill from the dock down the path.

Even though the generator disappointed us more than once, we were always somewhat ill-prepared. We had two vessels we pressed into service as needed: a newer plastic bucket and the galvanized metal fish gut bucket, which my dad used to collect the leftovers after filleting fish. We then tossed the bucket's contents on a nearby rocky island, where the birds had a feast. Despite its unfortunate moniker, the fish gut bucket had been well-cleaned. Still, we all agreed that we would use the plastic pail for our drinking water and the metal one to retrieve water for other purposes. Whenever we planned to walk down the hill, we were to check to see if the containers were empty and take them down to the dock to refill them.

I must be mindful of swinging the machete of truth without being careful of its power to wound.

One morning I headed down the path and saw my dad in the process of filling the buckets. My cheery greeting died in my throat when I saw what he was doing. My dad's knees were bad, and he had difficulty kneeling to scoop water. He had solved that problem by tying a rope to the handle of the metal pail. He tossed it into the water, then pulled it in all filled up. Then I watched as he carefully poured the water from the fish gut bucket into the plastic bucket and tossed the metal pail back out again.

When I confronted him about his clear violation of bucket protocol, Dad's explanation was that the plastic bucket bobbed on top of the water and wouldn't work with his rope contraption. My teenage self was horrified, and I promptly reported this infraction. My mom, a practical farm girl, didn't seem particularly surprised or bothered by the information. And my sister and I had to laugh because we had been drinking fish gut bucket water the whole time and never knew the difference.

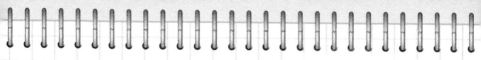

I learned that while honesty is usually the best policy, sometimes what we don't know can't hurt us.

My Uncle, My Hero

When my sister and I were about nine and ten, we visited my dad's brother and his wife in Wisconsin without our mom and dad—they were arriving from California later. We always loved visiting the farm where my dad grew up and spending time with his family.

We went on a little day trip to visit my aunt's aunt, whom we had never met before. She was a very nice lady, though a little gruff and intimidating in our young eyes. She had gone out of her way to prepare a special meal for us to enjoy for lunch: creamed lungs and dumplings.

My sister and I didn't know where to look when Great Aunt Matilda proudly set down a plate in front of each of us containing a dumpling the size of a man's fist covered with whitish strips of something in a cream gravy. Not wanting to insult our hostess, we valiantly tried to nibble at the dumpling, but the strips of lungs were beyond our capability. I tried a piece, and it really didn't have a bad flavor, but the spongy texture was too much for me.

Our uncle had mercy on our discomfort. When our hostess returned to the kitchen, he took our plates and scraped them onto his. When Great Aunt Matilda came back into the room and saw our clean plates, she promptly offered us another helping.

"Oh, we just couldn't," we said, truthfully. My sister and I couldn't because we didn't want any, and my uncle had just eaten three servings!

I learned that while honesty is usually the best policy, sometimes what we don't say can't hurt someone else.

Honesty, the Best Policy?

My understanding of honesty has evolved through the years. I'm no longer the vigilant tattletale I was as a child. I've come to realize that telling the truth with bad intentions is worse than pouring fish gut

bucket water into a plastic pail. Also, a lot of things masquerading as "truth" are really someone's deeply held opinions and do not always need to be shared.

Honesty is the best policy, but I have to begin by being honest with myself. Of course, there are times I will need to convey something difficult or unpleasant. However, I must be mindful of carelessly swinging the machete of truth without being careful of its power to wound. I have learned, too, that there is no reason to share every honest thought that pops into my head. Unless I have been asked for my opinion, I can keep some things to myself.

As the years go by and my memory isn't always the most reliable, I find that honesty is, more than ever, the best policy. My best chance of keeping my stories straight is to tell the truth—as far as I can recall.

Jesus, My Example

Jesus was a great advocate of telling the truth. So much of what he said began with the words, "I tell you the truth . . ." In his letter to the Ephesians, Paul said that when Christians become mature in their faith, they won't be victims of the deceitful scheming of men. Instead, by *speaking the truth in love*, [they] *may grow up in all things into Him who is the Head—Christ* (Ephesians 4:15 NKJV).

Honesty is the best policy when guided by the love of Christ. With his example before me, I will try to make wise decisions about what I say and what I keep to myself.

Procrastinate Tomorrow

by Robin Steinweg

*H*EY MOM, THEY called from work. I gotta go. Bye!" My son's voice drifted to me from upstairs, followed by the door's slam. *No. Oh, no.*

I took the stairs two at a time and launched myself outside, only to see my firstborn's car pull away. He didn't see me waving frantically from the middle of our street. I'd talk to him later about checking his rearview mirror more often.

The door slam had triggered a memory from earlier that morning when my husband asked me to run Important Errands for him. Important Financial Errands that couldn't wait.

"Consider it done," I'd said. I added my husband's errand to the end of my list. I'd have bags of time.

Now I stood in front of an empty garage viewing an empty neighborhood. Earlier, my younger son drove my car to work, and I had no one to call for a ride. I could walk the mile to the bank, but not by the time it closed.

My bike? There it was, in the rafters. The ladder would reach, but

I couldn't heft it down. My son's bike beckoned. Two and a half feet tall, it had fat tires and pegs for doing tricks. It might at least get me downtown in time.

I Was in Trouble

I swung my leg over the boy-bar, sat on the vinyl two-inch slice of rock called a seat, and wobbled down the driveway, the sun glinting off painted neon flames. Eight years since I'd ridden a bike, I couldn't keep to the side of the street. An oncoming car made me back-pedal to brake, but nothing happened. Legs circling furiously in reverse, I finally found the hand brakes. I'd gone half a block, and I was in trouble.

I've grown more sensitive to our Master Planner—I'll procrastinate tomorrow!

Had you stood on Broadway that afternoon, you'd have witnessed a middle-aged lady wheezing along, knees nearly knocking her chin, canvas tote whapping her leg at each rotation, breath coming in asthmatic gulps.

I accomplished the IFEs, walked the bike home, then sank into a hot Epsom salts bath. *There must be something redemptive in this.*

I Put Off the Most Important Task

Lord, is it a nudge to exercise more? As the bubbles and steam rose, I waited. I sensed it wasn't that simple. The thing I didn't want to think persisted. I'd put off the most important task until last. If only I'd done it right away. I squirmed. That morning I'd delivered another of my series of mother lectures on the sad outcomes of procrastination. "Do it now!" I told my sons. "If you do it right away, you won't have a chance to forget, and you won't have to worry if other things come up."

Oops.

Every ache that surfaced the next two days reminded me of the

chaos created by putting things off. This was not my first circus. It was only the most recent in a litany of procrastination. In fact, I had almost perfected it as an art form.

I'd started young. If asked to clean my room, my stock answer was, "I'll do it later." Later could be hours, days—even weeks. By high school, I'd hold off doing a term paper, pull an all-nighter, and complete it. It didn't help that I got A's on those last-minute-panic papers. It only fed the monster.

I Hid the Problem

I learned ways to hide my issue. Suppertime in fifteen minutes and no clue what to fix? No problem. Slap cheese on bread and grill it or crack eggs and scramble them. Valentine's Day left till the last minute and store shelves bare of cards? No problem. Heart-shaped pancakes make a unique valentine. Friends stop over and then need the bathroom? "One minute. Let me get towels out." I'd do it, then chip off globs of cement-like toothpaste I'd delayed wiping.

It may have appeared all was going well. But what a toll this took on my family! It's no fun to run out of gas when both credit card and checkbook are in my other purse, the contents of which I figured I'd swap out later. And to drag my husband from work forty-five minutes away to get me. No fun when the house smells of burnt plastic because I forgot I'd thrown food storage containers into the oven to hide them when unexpected guests arrived before I'd gotten around to washing them.

I needed to paint *Do it NOW* on my forehead.

Thoroughly ashamed of my habit, I opened my Bible for help. You might not find the word *procrastination* there, but God has plenty to say about it. While in Proverbs, I groaned over piled dishes and hardened toothpaste when I read that postponers will face hard labor. The actual term was *the slothful*, which made me wince.[1] Was I? Another

---

1. Proverbs 12:24, Proverbs 12:27, Proverbs 19:15

proverb highlighted a farmer who didn't plow on time. He'd look for food at the harvest, but there'd be none.[2] I'm no farmer, but I've rushed to the store for last-minute salad fixings, and they were out.

I cringed over Jesus's story about the five bridesmaids who brought their lamps and plenty of oil, while the other five didn't.[3] Those got locked out of the wedding reception because they weren't prepared. Wait. That wasn't procrastination. They didn't plan ahead. *Plan ahead!*

I Met the Master Planner

I saw God in a new way—as an amazing planner. He planned the perfect planet and atmosphere to sustain life for us. God instructs us and shows us the right way—and his plan is wonderful. I read that he knows each day scheduled for us before one of them has happened.[4] He formed a plan to redeem us through faith in Jesus's sacrifice even before Adam and Eve sinned.

I realized it's good to do things on time. But it isn't enough. It doesn't account for the unexpected. Instead of arriving on time but out of breath, I can leave earlier and drive with no sweating over stoplights. I can pick up extra groceries and make freezer-bag dinners so meals are prepared ahead. This allows for giving some away to sick or grieving friends. For the cost of five greeting cards, I can subscribe to a service that will schedule an unlimited number of cards to be emailed whenever I specify. I can purchase Christmas gifts all year and wrap them, as long as I make note of them.

I haven't mastered this. Just last fall I got too busy for Christmas shopping and then fell sick. With no energy for extras, once again, there were days of panic.

But I've grown more sensitive to the nudging of our Master Planner. I've grown more likely to procrastinate tomorrow!

---

2. Proverbs 20:4
3. Matthew 25:1–13
4. Psalm 139:16

Pay Attention, Dawn!

by Dawn Wilson

FOR MANY YEARS, I moved through life tuned out and inattentive, nearly oblivious to God's hand in it all. Not paying attention—or worse, ignoring warnings—became a bad habit. Consequently, I often acted foolishly or said silly things.

A Tuned-Out or Teachable Moment?

During my freshman year in high school, my dad's Navy assignment was in Iceland, and we lived off base in a Quonset hut. Accommodations were comfortable, but tight. Spreading my arms, I could touch one kitchen wall and cabinets on another. I decided to show off once and braced my hands against the wall and cabinets and swung my legs high like an Olympic gymnast on parallel bars. My dad warned me to be careful, but I tuned him out.

Suddenly, *thud!* Hitting the floor hard, I winced with pain. My entire family laughed. Then, paraphrasing Proverbs 16:18, my dad said, "Remember, Dawn, pride goes before a fall."

Lesson learned? No. I had many other teachable moments ahead.

While vacationing in Paris, I toured all the well-known sites with family members. We ate at a quaint French restaurant and shopped on the Champs-Élysées. Then we visited the Eiffel Tower. From the observation deck, I pointed out all the places we'd toured. Then I said, "Hey, where's the Eiffel Tower?"

Amused stares.

A Frenchman shook his head as my brother-in-law said, "Dawnie, you're on it."

I've often wondered: Does God laugh when, unfocused, I speak before I think?

I asked God to stir up a sense of wonder in my heart, and I promised to pay close attention.

The Blessing Basket

Over time, I've learned that I occasionally miss what God is up to because I don't ask him to show himself mighty on my behalf. But when I have asked, and when I stay alert and expectant for his reply, I marvel at his loving provision.

While traveling in my twenties with a national revival ministry, I stayed in people's homes. Before that ministry embraced a support-raising model, the director gave each team member ten dollars per week. I was grateful because I received no financial help from home, but the stipend didn't stretch far enough. Concerned one morning, I prayed, "Lord, are you going to care for me, or do I need to leave?" I listed my needs, then packed for travel to the next church.

Another girl and I were assigned to stay with an elderly lady. She led us to a basement guestroom. What I saw next made me cry. On each of our beds sat a large basket. As we gratefully unloaded them, we found hairspray, mouthwash, toothpaste, breath mints, deodorant, thank you cards, and so much more—even an envelope with cash "For something I may have missed."

The blessing basket was tangible evidence that, although I may not always pay attention, God does!

A Year of Wonder

After a diagnosis of multiple myeloma, I regretted that I hadn't taken life as seriously as I could have to that point. Floating through life without paying attention to God's direction had consequences. As I lamented my lack of direction and lost opportunities, I knew I didn't want to miss anything again. When a friend mentioned how renewing a sense of wonder about God encouraged her to take life more seriously, I asked God to stir up a sense of wonder in my heart. I promised to pay close attention. I chose the word *wonder* as my word for the year.

In January, I focused on *Wonder and Worship*. Wonder regarding God can lead us to worship him. As the Israelites declared, *Who is like you, majestic in holiness, awesome in glorious deeds, doing wonders?* (Exodus 15:11 ESV).

In February, I considered *Wonder and Worth*. God's assessment of my worth is deeper than the world's opinions. I evaluated my schedule and changed priorities as I saw the life-building purposes of the One who loves me.

I studied *Wonder and Wisdom* in March. Scripture says the fear of the Lord is the foundation of wisdom.[5] I determined to fear God—to view him with wonder and reverential awe—so I could grow in wisdom.

In April, I considered *Wonder and My Walk with God*. As I pondered God's holiness, the Holy Spirit gave me new attitudes, behaviors, and daily habits.

May's topic was the *Wonder of My Witness*. I was astounded that God calls sinners who are transformed—but still sinners—to share the gospel. I paid closer attention to the people he brought into my life so I could share the gospel or minister to them.

In June, I studied *Wonder and My Work*. I tend to be self-sufficient, but the truth is, apart from the Lord, I can do nothing.[6] I considered how God is my sufficiency during my workweek.

---

5. Proverbs 9:10
6. John 15:5

July's *Wonder and My Wishes* surprised me. With misguided thinking, I thought, "If I desire something, it must not be of God." God opened my eyes! The psalmist said, *Delight yourself in the L*ORD, *and he will give you the desires of your heart* (Psalm 37:4 ESV).

In August, I studied *Wonder and My Words*. God gave me courage, and as I shared stories about his love and faithfulness with my family and friends, they were helped and encouraged.

I studied *Wonder and My Wealth* in September, observing how gratitude for God's provision and the wise use of resources can produce lasting kingdom fruit that honors God.

In October, *Wonder and My Watchfulness* gave me a fresh perspective on my diagnosis. I read Randy Alcorn's book *Heaven* and focused on Scriptures about my home in heaven and the Lord's return. God created a greater desire to know and please him.

The Overflow of Wonder

After ten months of focusing on wonder, my heart overflowed! Paying attention paid off.

I spent November praising God, focusing particularly on the wonders of his creation. I sat beneath the stars and imagined God saying, "I made this for you!" David A. Steen's book *God of Wonders* helped me pay closer attention to God's creativity.

In December, I focused on giving, serving, and encouraging others. I gave Christmas gifts that included the word *wonder* and wrote about *My Wonder Adventure*.

Over that year, I discovered the distracting world steals our wonder. Sometimes our unfocused thoughts hinder it, and Satan conspires against it—but my year of wonder ultimately fostered a new habit of noticing. I now pay attention to things I missed before, and I see God's hand in life's events, both big and small.

The Thinking Chair

by Sandy Lipsky

*T*HE ARRIVAL OF my favorite chair almost led to marriage counseling. The recliner poses a picture of peacefulness these days, nestled in a corner of my tiny office. Gazing at it, you might think it descended from heaven like a stork delivery. Both of those are tall tales.

Satisfying Quest

As a writer, I wanted a place to ponder. I searched for months to find the perfect "thinking chair" for my office. An unhurried pursuit paid off months later. My daughter and I strolled into the local outlet store and spotted a recliner with gray and white herringbone upholstery. We took turns sinking into the luxury of its cushions and unanimously agreed the hunt was over. Before offering my credit card, I asked the salesperson if the chair would fit in my SUV once it arrived at the warehouse. She assured me it would. The estimated date of delivery was eight weeks.

Months later, I received a phone call from the furniture store. My purchase awaited retrieval at last. Excitement ensued. According to

my estimation, the process of picking up and delivering to my office should take two hours. My husband, Jon, and I headed to the warehouse the following Saturday. An afternoon memorial service allowed minimal leeway of time. We left our home soon after breakfast. This would give us time to change our clothes and shower before the funeral.

Unexpected Troubles

The drive took forty minutes. Soon after our arrival, two employees carried my purchase through the warehouse traffic doors. They deposited the massive box behind our vehicle. Jon said to me, "It's not going to fit."

Perseverance is hard, but its reward is substantial.

"The store employee assured me the chair would divide into two pieces."

One of the workers looked at our trunk and then at the box. He removed the wrap and cardboard. The men picked up the naked chair with the intent of pushing it into our trunk. Unsuccessful, they came to the same conclusion my husband had seconds earlier.

Without pause, one of the young men said, "Let's try another angle." It still did not fit. Three pickup trucks pulled in behind us while the employees worked on our space issue. The helpful staff member did not seem to notice the growing line and stared at the ground. Finally, he lifted his head and said, "You have a few options." We agreed a rental truck made the most sense and drove to the nearest location. The first business proved a dead end. By the third stop, we found a suitable rig.

We parked our car at the rental store and headed back to the furniture warehouse. Once we arrived, we waited in line several more minutes to have the recliner loaded into the U-Haul. The behemoth chair now looked like a shrimp in the sea of trailer space.

Giddy, we drove the twenty miles to our house. The next step in our trek proved to be the most fun. We'd bought shoulder dolly straps

at the truck rental. While my mate lifted the chair out of the trailer, I read the directions. We placed the straps over our shoulders and under the chair. It took minimal effort to lift the chair across the driveway and through our front door. I plopped into the chair, melting in the cloudlike softness. My husband scooched past me in the entryway.

"There's no way we can get this up the stairs."

His stern glare quieted my suggestion of removing the rail to widen the space. Expressing disappointment that we'd missed the funeral, Jon charged me with figuring out the problem. He disappeared down the basement stairs.

Necessary Miracle

Crazy thoughts flashed in my mind. Why not leave the chair in the entryway? I could greet guests while comfortably seated. If family needed my attention, I would be easy to find. Although ridiculous, this chair had won my affections. It would be painful to return.

I decided to call the salesperson. She was at the store and remembered me. Her solution involved asking co-workers to disassemble the display chair. Once apart, she would call me with instructions. Too nervous to wait by the phone, I cleaned the kitchen and prayed. I didn't see my husband again until dinner.

Closing time for the furniture store approached, and the long-awaited call from the furniture employee did not come. I called her. She apologized for her slight and said with a matter-of-fact tone, "The chair can't be unassembled. You have three days to return it and get your money back."

Determined to find a way to get the chair up the stairs, I opened a kitchen drawer and pulled out a tape measure. No matter which angles I measured, the chair was too big. My hopes dwindled. I prepared our evening meal.

We ate dinner in silence and went to bed.

Before church the next morning, I noticed the chair on its side in an adjacent room to our entryway. My husband, with a screwdriver

in hand, stared at the underside. His computer sat on the floor next to him. His eyes looked back and forth from the chair to the screen. Without saying a word, I went upstairs to change clothes. When I came down the steps minutes later, I noticed a section of the chair lying separate from the base. We left to attend Sunday service.

Once home, we finished another silent meal.

Finally, my husband whispered, "I'm going to get your chair upstairs." I recognized the resolution in his voice. Too scared to watch, I went into our bathroom and shut the door. I asked the Lord to give him strength and protection while I clutched my phone.

With brute force and a steel will, Jon carried part of the chair over his head and set it down outside my office door. When I peeked out of my hiding place, the chair rested on the landing.

Indebted to my beloved's dauntlessness, I grabbed the base to help in the last stage of the journey. Astounded at the proximity of the chair to its final haven, I cheered. As we lifted in tandem, Jon looked at me and said, "It won't fit."

Difficult Perseverance

"We are so close," I lamented. I heard a sharp exhale through closed teeth and then a request for a tool. The hinges pulled away from the door frame with each forceful turn of the screwdriver. We balanced the door against an adjacent wall and then pushed aside an obstructing bookshelf. Without a word, my husband and I forced the chair through the opening and shimmied it to the corner. We left the room together.

Two weeks passed before I sat in the chair. Even more time for Jon. The raw memory of sacrifice and determination brought a holy attitude toward this piece of furniture. I didn't feel worthy of the gift.

Now, whenever I sit in my thinking chair, I reflect on the drama of its arrival. Hardship produced treasure. It's impossible to count the life lessons learned after thirty-five years of marriage, but this recent lesson holds a special place in my heart. Perseverance is hard, but its reward is substantial.

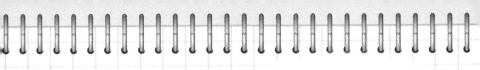

Finding My Way

by Charlaine Martin

*Y*AY, THIS IS fun!" my three kids and their friends cheered from the back. But my heart screamed, *WE'RE LOST!* They had no idea how scared I felt. With a white-knuckle grip on my steering wheel, I pondered which way to turn. Directionally impaired me had mixed up my friend's instructions to get home and turned right instead of left. What a big mistake!

I was mortified about getting lost. I couldn't remember verbal directions except for the last turn. GPS and smartphones only existed in science fiction then. We received free maps from AAA that sat on my desk. If a GPS had existed, I wouldn't have been in this mess!

Unexpected Adventure

I'd set play dates with two moms from church, Marie and Sondra, that summer since our kids needed something to do. Our rambunctious youngsters loved playing together while we chatted over coffee. It was Marie's turn to host the play date, and she had errands nearby. I picked up Sondra's kids after lunch, then met Marie in the church's parking lot.

I'd never been to her home, so I followed her there. It was the perfect plan—until I tried navigating home.

After wandering the countryside for over an hour, I spied the shores of Lake Erie. *Whoa! Why do I see the lake?* I panicked and turned around. It was the opposite direction from home. *Why didn't I grab that map before I left?* I groaned. *God, please help me!*

> God listens to our tearful pleas of desperation and gives us help in our time of need.

I tried doing that north-south-east-west thing my husband always did. Yet, my feeble attempts brought me to a crossroads with a bar and phone booth in the middle of nowhere. Anxiety gripped me. Suddenly I had a bright idea to call my husband! He could figure this out. So, I pulled up to the phonebooth and hopped out. While the kids squealed with glee inside, I put a quarter in one of the phones to call Don. Surely, he could get me back home—right?

I dialed his work number. "Honey." I sniffled. "I'm soooo lost. Can you help me get back home?"

"Where are you?" Showing his concern, he pondered aloud, "How in the world did Char end up near Lake Erie?"

"I'm at a phone booth on a crossroads at Such-n-Such Bar," I replied, hoping he could route me home.

"What are the intersecting roads?"

Oh, my logical engineer-husband. This is why I called him.

"I'll look for it on a map," he said.

"Let me see." I stepped out to read the road signs and then told him.

While he checked his map, I used the second payphone to call

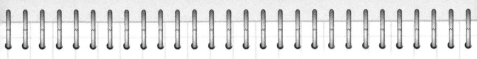

Sondra, to let her know what happened so she wouldn't be concerned about her boys. It was a relief when she told me not to worry and that she'd pray for us.

After hanging up with her, I settled the kids down because our van had begun to rock from their jumping around. Finally, Don came back with the route I needed. "By the way, how *did* you get *there?*"

I explained, "I forgot the first turn from Marie's directions."

Happy to have clear instructions, I navigated to the interstate. Lo and behold, I had traveled two hours east out of my way. The correct route was only forty-five minutes west. At twilight, I pulled into Sondra's driveway. Her boys hopped out and thanked me for their fun adventure. I wish I could have been as giddy about it as they were. She came out her front door and hugged me. Frazzled, I felt so grateful to be home.

I discovered we'd been near crime-riddled sections of Toledo. Why did I think my warped navigational abilities could work like my husband's? After this, I learned to keep a local map in the van with me and pray.

Delayed Graduation

I hadn't graduated from God's Life Lessons Academy yet. He knew my fear of getting lost was debilitating. I still had much to learn before I could drive alone wherever necessary.

Years later, after Don traded his lab coat for a pulpit, God continued to build my trust in navigation tools and him. When I needed to find a hospital in Pittsburgh, I discovered that old cities share street names spelled differently followed by Street, Avenue, or Boulevard. God sent a woman pushing a baby stroller to help me when my GPS set for Center Street took me to an abandoned warehouse defaced by gang graffiti. I drove around trying to start over but always ended up at the same place. When I saw her, I stopped. "Where is UPMC Hospital? I'm lost."

She cautiously looked around, then came a bit closer. As we talked, I found out I needed Centre Avenue, not Center Street. What a difference—such a picky navigational device! That sweet angel directed me to the hospital.

Fitting Trade

Years later, my youngest matured from a child in a car seat into a college student in the driver's seat. She went to see her dad at the hospital in Pittsburgh and took me with her. After our visit, we hugged Don. "Thanks for visiting with me. Love you both!" he smiled. Then she and I walked to the parking garage to go home.

She followed our GPS. I'd learned to *love* these devices. As she drove, I rested in my seat. Eventually, we came to an awkward intersection at a traffic light. Pittsburgh is notorious for odd-angled streets. "Turn far right," the GPS instructed. Confused, we pulled over.

"Right, second right, or third right. Which one is far right?" I asked my daughter. It wasn't the first one, so we guessed, hoping we were correct. A paper map sure would've been handy. Perplexed, we found ourselves on dark, rain-glistened backroads.

At one point in this not-so-grand adventure, we climbed a steep, twisty, narrow road up a mountain with no guard rails. Stars for streetlights. Rachel, wide-eyed, had a white-knuckle grip on the steering wheel. I kept track of our tires at the edge of the road.

Suddenly, I remembered a popular cartoon with a sweet, clumsy dog towing a camper behind his car up such a road. The camper swung off the cliff by a signpost, then back on as he rounded the bend. The thought made me laugh and yodel.

Annoyed, Rachel snapped, "Stop it, Mom. I'm gonna wet my pants!"

"Sorry, Sweetie." I sheepishly apologized, then prayed. After reaching the top, we spiraled back down. Then we stumbled upon a good road, found a couple of towns on the GPS, and headed in their

direction. Hoping to find help, we noticed shuttered businesses as we drove through. Then an onramp to a familiar highway appeared, and we spied a truck stop.

"Yay!" I cheered.

Rachel sprinted to find the bathroom while I found our route on the GPS. We arrived safely home two hours later.

Successful Lessons

God has a crazy sense of humor in his Life Lessons Academy. Each situation could've been unfortunate. We relied on a device that failed, yet God never fails. God set me up with the tools and support I needed for when I needed to drive solo. My anxiety shut me down, but humor quelled my fears. My greatest discovery? God listens to our tearful pleas of desperation and gives us help in our time of need.

Living Lullabies of Love

by Becki James

$\mathcal{I}$ SAT ON THE edge of the hospital bed, holding the hand of my twenty-nine-year-old daughter. She had braved the knife, opting to slice open her body to unwrap the gift within her. I marveled that many would consider her work done—the months of pregnancy completed. But sitting there, looking at her post-op, I saw the lifelong labor that grew from that incision. Behind the closed door, muffled call-bells hummed, and footsteps padded back and forth. I was glad for the dimmed lights and moon rising high. Resting there, with much weariness, we met eyes—speaking the silent complexities of being mothers.

"Well, Mom, we made it through the first day."

I nodded. That we did. My son-in-law had gone home to tuck their toddler in bed, and I stayed to help ease the toil of the first hours. All was well. I smiled, inhaling the goodness of the moment, not wanting it to end. But I understood her need for rest. I knew it was time to settle my little girl in bed before going home.

Teetering on the edge of her mattress, I shifted my weight much like days gone by. Her fingers felt small enfolded in mine. I gave them

a little squeeze, stirring more memories of the bitty fingers that once latched around my pinky. Lullabies echoed in my mind. Tattered storybook pages turned. The scent of freshly bathed skin and fuzzy hair resurfaced. Years had ticked past me, consumed in the race to maturity. My child had grown. So had I.

Now, donned in the gowns of motherhood, we bowed our heads in praise to God.

"The Lord prevails," I felt my voice break as the words came. "This is what Sherayah's name means—and you, O God, have prevailed." Tears pressed hard against my eyelids, forcing a downward stream of gratitude to fall wet upon our intertwined fingers. "Your purpose, heavenly Father, prevailed when she began life weighing just three pounds."

I gulped at the lump forming in my throat. "And surviving prematurity, Lord, to this day. Your love has prevailed over her—and me—all these years. Thank you, Father, for your love and for new life."

God's peace pours over us like a silken balm, cleansing what is wounded.

Prevailing Peace

Yes, the Lord prevails. He always has and always will reign victorious in his purpose for each of us. Knowing this has been the basis of my peace when troubles arise. Peace is the gift that empowers us when we honor God's presence. God's peace pours over us like a silken balm, cleansing what is wounded. It is described as a state of being calm and free from stress.

I think I would go a step further to say peace is a state of calm *despite* the presence of stress. Someone who holds peace is hard to argue with. Their strength of composure dislodges fear, dethroning anxieties.

Thirty years ago, predicting premature labor was nearly impossible, let alone the likelihood of a healthy infant making her debut three months underdeveloped. With sudden pain gripping my abdomen,

my daughter had proclaimed her arrival. Flipping the switch for critical care protocols, the medical team aimed to postpone her birth. Contractions continued, and undeniable threats escalated—the worst being the possible death of one or both of us.

On top of that, the nearest neonatal facility was ninety minutes away, and a severe snowstorm had grounded the transport helicopter. Yet, even in the face of urgency and potential death, I experienced peace. What I felt came from knowing God was with me.

Prevailing Trust

Somewhere along the way, the Lord got my attention through this Scripture: Trust in the LORD with all your heart, and do not lean on your own understanding. In all your ways acknowledge him, and he will make straight your paths (Proverbs 3:5–6 ESV). These words encouraged me and stuck with me. Trusting God does not mean disregarding those with skill or knowledge. Trusting God means recognizing him as my ultimate source of confidence and having faith in his plan for my good because he is good.

After bouncing me from the delivery unit to recovery several times in the course of a week, the medical team determined that an untimely birth was imminent. My labor intensified despite being probed, poked, and prescribed every treatment available. Finally, a panel of nine doctors lined my room to give me the game plan. Heavy with medication, I cupped my hand over one eye to keep the room from spinning. When they paused to assess my comprehension, my response brought looks of surprise. "If God wants this child to be born," I asserted, "she will be born regardless of anything you try."

A younger doctor snapped back, "Do you have any idea what premature birth entails?" The fact is, at that time, I did not. But I knew my Lord. I knew he wouldn't fail me. I chose to trust him and lean on his presence.

Prevailing Love

I have watched God work in my life for more than forty years. If God

was not trustworthy, I would have dumped him by now. His love is eternal—not short-lived. Time and again, my love for him has faltered. But he countered with unmatched devotion, confirming his faithfulness to me.

I no longer doubt God's love. With his tender track record, I cannot fight the evidence. King David testified to this, saying, *You make known to me the path of life; in your presence there is fullness of joy; at your right hand are pleasures forevermore* (Psalm 16:11 esv). When I struggle with circumstances that make me want to hide, I find refuge and renewed joy in God's presence. Because of this confidence, with awe and affection, I call him Lord.

Prevailing Lord

I chose my daughter's name long before I knew the power of its meaning. Trusting in this Lord who prevails has been a process. I still zigzag, wobbling in my own reasoning. But when I acknowledge his purposes, my perception clears into sustaining peace. I realize leaning on my own understanding regularly tips me off-balance. But putting confidence in God's character and living in his presence has helped me rest in his plan.

Yes, the Lord prevails. Nearly three decades ago, the Lord provided a neonatal team that stood ready to feed breathing tubes into an undeveloped infant the minute she entered this world. She spent fifty-eight days in that NICU before coming home attached to a cardiac monitor and oxygen for the first six months of her life.

This year, I sat with my hand in hers. A mother just like me. Beside us, snugged in cotton cocoons, the rhythm of tiny breaths lulled us with sweet contentment. Capped in pink and blue, a gorgeous girl and a beautiful boy had successfully navigated the strenuous transition from womb to world. Twins, weighing four pounds each, were in God's good plan for my little girl. And once again, the Lord answered my prayers for the safe delivery of life. The circle of his faithfulness sings a lullaby of love to me. Great is the Lord who prevails!

A Caricature of Impatience

by Sally Ferguson

*Y*OU KNOW THAT sinking feeling of getting caught? That place in the pit of your belly that says, "The gig's up"? My stomach plummeted one day when I was pulled over for speeding. I'll share more on that later, but this feeling had been building up for a while. I felt yanked in every direction, and my need for control mocked me at every turn.

When I think about it now, I realize how ludicrous that sounds. However, the frame of reference from which I operated said I had to be in charge. When I lost control, I became impatient. And impatience manifested itself in four different ways: anger, conflict, getting ahead of God's timing, and a need for disciplinary action from the Lord. I needed to learn to rein in my tongue and let the Lord have charge of my plans.

Boiling Before Cooling

I never knew I was churlish until I had children. It's as if an inactive volcano came to a boil under volatile situations. When a variety of

personalities live in one house, there's bound to be friction. Still, I took it as an affront to my ideal of a perfect family life.

The day it all came to a head, I threw a chair across the bedroom. No child was in harm's way of my temper tantrum, but they witnessed my outburst. If a cartoonist could capture me at that moment, they would draw a wild-eyed, hair-flying mama hanging from the rafters. I had to deescalate—and fast—before squashing little personalities. I needed perspective, and I needed to ask forgiveness.

Flexing Plans

In my need for control, I seemed to have an agenda others couldn't fill. They couldn't meet my expectations, nor did they have a clue of what they were. Confrontation occurs whenever my perception of a situation gets blown way out of proportion to what actually happened. That sort of conflict happened recently when I got upset at a family member for one thing, then piled on years of perceived offenses. It was a no-win situation.

If a cartoonist drew me then, I would look like a raving lunatic. What did I need to learn? Don't let the little things build up into big things. I had to let go of expecting others to fit into my narrative. I was living proof that a *hot-tempered person starts fights* (Proverbs 15:18 NLT).

When a variety of personalities live in one house, there's bound to be friction.

Getting Ahead of God's Timing

I was always in a hurry. Inevitably, Sunday mornings turned chaotic—a lost shoe, a diaper that needed to be changed (again), the baby spit up on the only clean clothes that fit. I was overwhelmed. At the same time, I took on more responsibilities outside of the home in an effort to find

validation for the lonely soul inside of me. I was overscheduled, which resulted in being frustrated and having an unpredictable disposition.

My cartoon for this would have me tapping my foot impatiently while looking at my watch. I was in a hurry for God to work in my circumstances. What I needed was to slow down and enjoy the moment with my kids.

Embracing God's Discipline

The day I saw the cherry top lights flashing in my rearview mirror, I knew it was time for a reckoning. A little voice in the car seat asked, "Mommy, why did that police officer stop us?"

How could I answer? It wasn't my child's fault we were late for piano lessons. It was a perfect storm of lost music, jackets, the phone ringing, and stoplights. An avalanche of tension caught up to me there by the side of the road. A speeding ticket became God's disciplinary action to teach me humility and bring me in check. Color me humbled and call it a day.

I was looking for love in all the wrong places and still coming up empty. I wanted validation for being a good wife, a good mom, a good cook, a good women's ministry leader, a good room mom at school . . . that's a lot of goods for one person to carry on her shoulders. My *goods backpack* got too heavy and spilled out over every *good* thing in life. When I learned to let God have jurisdiction, I found out he enables me to have endurance and patience. And those are beautiful qualities for a mom to embrace.

Overcoming the Roadblocks

A man who could not walk was desperate to get to Jesus. He enlisted the help of his friends, but they were still roadblocked. Mark 2:4 says, *And when they could not come near Him because of the crowd, they uncovered the roof where He was. So when they had broken through, they let down the bed on which the paralytic was lying* (NKJV).

At times we cannot get to Jesus. Crowded thoughts, busyness, and the daily cares of life block access. Moms of toddlers can relate—they can't even make a trip to the bathroom without someone hollering, "Mommy!" Moms of teens know it well too. I operated as a taxi mom, with my minivan as my office. Women climbing the ladder in the workforce can relate. There aren't enough hours in a day to get everything done. How do we make an opening in a jampacked life?

It takes some creativity to find ways to be alone with the Lord. When my two were little, sometimes middle-of-the-night Bible study was my only opportunity to have a quiet house for my quiet time with God. Like the paralyzed man who had to get creative to get to God, we can overcome whatever is blocking access to Jesus.

He had to rely on some friends to dig through layers of roofing material to meet his need. How do I rely on my friends? What layers of mistrust and misunderstanding do I need to dig through to get to genuine relationship? How am I a friend to others? Do I make excuses for not making room for them in my life?

The man's friends lowered the mat to make Jesus accessible. I am often paralyzed and need to be humbled before the Lord. I need my friends to carry me when fear, inadequacy, and darkness of soul stymie my healing. Friends bring me to Jesus in my helplessness to be helped by him. And I am there for my friends. We're learning to be available in every emotion-laden season of life. I hope my present cartoon self would depict me surrounded by friends.

I was angry, conflicted, and running ahead of God, so he allowed opportunities for correction. It involved repeated warning signs—a painful lesson I've never forgotten. These days I'm looking for love by filling up my empty tank at the feet of Jesus. My ideal patient and carefree caricature would look like a gal driving down life's highway with hair blowing in the wind. She has a smile on her face and peace in her heart!

Twelve Years to Truth

by Hally Wells

OURNALS, DIARIES, AND old planners are delightful treasures to retain and review as the years blow by. I am currently 60 percent through my second ten-year journal, and looking back at prior years on any given date inspires various emotions. Sometimes, I rejoice because life is better. Occasionally, I mourn for people no longer with me.

From time to time, I recognize how much I have learned. Having experiences where I'm inspired by something I've written in private is one thing. Reading and experiencing thoughts about my words that were published to the public—and realizing I'm not as smart as I thought when I authored the piece—is quite another!

That was my experience when one of my early published devotions came to mind long after I wrote it about a dozen years earlier. Cringe-worthy also comes to mind!

Magic or Muscle

The devotion was entitled "Magic or Muscle." I felt the title was cute, and there were a few funny lines, but my overall message was serious.

I wrote with authority and conviction about what it looks like to be a good mom. While I acknowledged that moms aren't made on a manufacturing line and come in various personalities and mom styles, the best parenting pros toil and put in the time. My confidence and certitude regarding what I then understood of parenting have often been shaken since I wrote that devotion.

I was rockin' the process! But, I wasn't wrong about the process, I was wrong about the results.

Back then, I was a mother of two elementary children. I spoke briefly about how my opinions about parenting had changed since I'd been in high school. I explained that as a teenager, I had been certain I didn't want children. I somehow faced my fears regarding the physical challenges and the chances that I might have a "silly looking and simple-minded rabbit-out-of-a-hat kind of kid."

Yes, I had come to *know* that this parenting thing was a matter of effort rather than anything mystical—an issue of work rather than luck. My assertion and reassurance, though more implied than stated outright to readers, was that those moms and dads who really did their jobs as parents would surely be successful in raising happy, healthy, well-adjusted, accomplished, Christian people. Mic drop!

All the Things

In case any were uncertain what those secrets to success were, I described them in my piece. I explained that industrious moms are pleased when their kids land in the hard teacher's classroom. They know that even though the homework will be daunting, the learning will double. In teaching chores to children, I acknowledged that the task of cleaning

32

house often takes twice as long when you're soliciting help from kids, but it's time well spent to help them develop a superior work ethic. I cited multiple extra-curricular activities, nightly prayers, and church attendance as essential elements of praiseworthy parenting.

I approached parenting with my naturally practical perspective, doing each of those things just as I had written. I was rockin' the process!

I've learned I wasn't wrong about the process. I was wrong about the results.

Rude Awakening

Over the next several years, my children went from spelling bees to science fairs, 4-H to FFA, field trips to friend groups, and things became much more complicated. In those years, while one child was sharing everything with me, another was unable or unwilling to communicate much of anything to me. I missed the damage done by devices in my home and overlooked the impact of early trauma.

While one of my offspring became rather thick-skinned and almost impenetrable when facing negative peer influences, the other was exceedingly eager to please and vulnerable to those same types of individuals. One was resilient. One was broken and in need of repair.

We addressed each blow of bad behavior and each shock of sadness with a proposed solution, a new tactic, a change in the conversation, treatment, consequences, and on and on. My husband and I continued to do the work, though it wasn't the type we had ever anticipated. We were reacting, trying everything we could to repair our child.

Throughout our journey, which included a wilderness experience and a therapeutic boarding school, we met others like ourselves—parents who seemed to have all the resources, smarts, and tools to parent well. Group counseling sessions and parent training brought us into contact with beautiful, loving, diverse, and disillusioned families.

The kid situations within those families were unique, yet we shared experiences among us. We had a shared desperation too. Often, I've interacted with parents in online groups on the very same journey. It has been an adventure in extreme parenting! Where "doing all the things" was equivalent to a community college class, the new skills we learned amounted to a doctorate level course!

Righteous Awareness

We expect our greatest times of growth and learning to happen when we're young. Yet, wise men and women have recognized the value and benefits of continuing to seek knowledge throughout our lives. We find as we grow older that though we've gained significant knowledge, there remains much more we don't understand. I wasn't seeking to learn anything new when my beliefs about parenting were turned upside down. However, I most certainly did.

What I learned is that sometimes the success, happiness, and behavior of a child do not reflect their parents' effort, competency, love, and performance. That's big! There is no magic formula guaranteed to result in a mentally healthy young person. Many mothers and fathers do their absolute best to love their son or daughter and endure their own scary parenting journeys, grieving for their struggling child.

When I wrote that devotion twelve years ago, I didn't think it might hurt someone. I didn't view it as judgmental or condemning in any way, but I now have knowledge and life experience that cause me to view the words differently. I suggested what I believed to be wonderful practices for parents, and I stand by those. What I didn't recognize then is that so many are doing fabulous jobs at the work of parenting without the result they have earned. I know now that just because a child is faltering and flailing, it does not mean their parents have done the same.

DNA, trauma, personalities, resiliency, peers, learning disabilities, self-esteem, and a myriad of other factors combine to create the persons our children grow to be, and it "ain't always a cakewalk." My child is healthy now. My child is happy, building a relationship with Jesus, nurturing friendships, and developing career skills. I am blessed. I have worked very hard. I am an excellent momma, but I know the truth. Prayers helped me endure and my child survive. And while I asserted that there was no luck or mystery involved in effective parenting—there just might be!

That devotion was one of well over one hundred that I wrote for the website over a period of several years. I hope readers of that one article forgive any hurt that I caused them. I am wiser now, and I am grateful for the lesson.

When Obedience Is Hard

by Natasha Lynn Daniels

*H*AVE YOU EVER struggled to obey God's will because you didn't like what he asked you to do? I wasn't ready to trust God when he led me in an unexpected direction.

A Season for Everything

My husband and I adopted our five children. We were blessed with our son Micah when he was six weeks old. He was a local adoption. Our other four children are a sibling group we adopted from an orphanage in Ukraine. I knew from the beginning that God had called me to homeschool.

I'd homeschooled Micah from the start, and his graduation was approaching. I wasn't ready to let him go. King Solomon said in Ecclesiastes that there is a time for everything,[7] but I didn't think it was the time for graduation.

I sensed the Lord whisper, *Natasha, trust me.*

---

7. Ecclesiastes 3:1

"I'm not ready. He's my baby, the one who made me a mommy. Lord, how do I let him go?"

As the Lord dealt with me to release Micah, he also urged me to place my other two boys in school. To be honest, I wrestled with the Lord. How could he want this? I placed my identity in being a homeschool mom, and the fear of change was crippling. Allowing the lies of the Enemy to consume me, I felt like a failure thinking I could no longer school all five of my children well.

I also struggled with the thought of letting down my fellow home-school moms by going to "the other side." Putting my boys in school during a pandemic could not be God's will for our family. Surely, I was hearing him wrong.

I moved forward with my plans to homeschool all five of my children for the 2020–2021 school year. Well, the Lord has a way of getting our attention.

When I surrendered my plans for his, I found peace.

As the school year progressed, Andy* struggled academically and needed more of my time. James* excelled academically and wasn't challenged enough. Micah stopped giving me his best, and my time was stretched with the boys. I was so focused on these three boys that I wasn't giving my girls the best of me during their elementary years.

I sought the Lord for guidance, and again he whispered into my heart. *Natasha, graduate Micah and put the boys in school.* Oh, how my heart quaked.

Additionally, Andy and James wanted to play sports, but homeschool students find it hard to participate on the school's sports teams. Micah loves music, and we provided lessons to nurture his gift.

The Lord was nudging me to enjoy the gifts and talents of my other boys as well. Once more, I cried out, "Lord, what about the influence of their peers in school?"

I heard him say, *Natasha, do you trust me?*

"Yes, Lord, I trust you."

Natasha, do you trust me?

Yes, Lord, I trust you."

A third time. *Natasha, do you trust me?*

"Yes, Lord, I trust you."

I recalled the passage in the Bible when Jesus asked Peter three times if he loved him, and each time Peter responded, "Yes."[8]

Jesus reminded Peter that if he loved him, then Peter should feed his sheep. God doesn't ask us if we love and trust him because he needs to know. He knows our hearts already. God asks us because we need to recognize the truth. *Natasha, if you love me, then trust me.*

The Battle Belongs to the Lord

The word the Lord gave me for the year 2020 was confident. The Scripture he gave me was Philippians 1:6. Being confident of this very thing, that He who has begun a good work in you will complete it until the day of Jesus Christ (NKJV).

The Lord led me to study the book of Joshua. Honestly, I didn't want to read Joshua. I already knew about the walls of Jericho. But the Lord laid out so much more than the walls of Jericho. He displayed my word *confident* throughout the book of Joshua and reminded me to be strong and courageous in all things.

In Joshua, chapter 7, Ai defeated the Israelites because of Achan's sin. Joshua cried out to the Lord, asking why this happened and why God had brought them across the Jordan. The Lord told Joshua to get up and asked him why he was lying on his face. The Lord reminded

8. John 21:15–19

him Israel had sinned and broken his covenant. The Lord also pointed out they stole some of the items he commanded must be set apart for him. And not only had they stolen these consecrated items, but they lied about it and hid them among their own belongings.

The heaviness of schooling all my children was still hovering. Crying out for help, I sensed the Lord using Joshua 7 to speak similarly to me as he did to Joshua. *Natasha, Get up! Why are you still moaning about this? I indicated what you were to do, but you disobeyed. Not only did you disobey, but you made excuses instead of being obedient.* Ouch!

I related with Joshua in this moment and knew it was time to surrender to the Lord's will and trust that he would complete the good work he started in me.

The Surrender to His Will

> *Yet God has made everything beautiful for its own time. He has planted eternity in the human heart, but even so, people cannot see the whole scope of God's work from beginning to end.* (Ecclesiastes 3:11 NLT)

With complete surrender, I transitioned our three boys. God's peace enveloped me. I was free from the lies of the Enemy. God's presence washed over me, and his fierce love met me in my brokenness and disobedience.

God reminded me that he loves my family and children more than I do. They are his. He lent them to me. He knows what is best for them and their future. Being honest with myself, I knew I had put more trust in what I could do than in what he could do. Change is hard. Obedience is hard. But God is faithful.

Though I could not see the whole scope of God's work from beginning to end, I chose to trust and believe. As I said goodbye to a part of who I was and what our family looked like, he reminded me that he goes before us to clear the path, he walks behind us to protect us, and he walks beside us, whispering which way to go. I still grieve what was,

but I hold fast to his principles in Ecclesiastes. He was faithful then, and he is faithful now.

A New Season Blooms

Micah works full-time and lives on his own. Our other two boys have attended public school for over a year. Andy is finding his way, James is on the football team, and I'm soaking in being with my girls as we continue to homeschool.

Life is nothing like I thought it would be, but I am learning to embrace this new season. Obedience is toilsome, but God makes all things beautiful in his time. When I surrendered my plans for his, I found peace.

* Name changed.

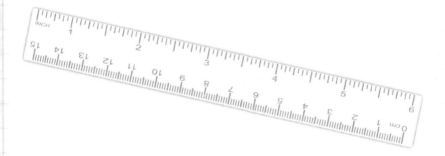

Who Do I Serve?

by Teresa Janzen

*R*UMPLED CLOTHING CLUNG to my body as sweat beads formed on my forehead. Finally, after three days of travel to my new home at the village hospital, it was time to shower.

Willing to Serve

A flowering banana tree shaded the tin-walled structure, which had a gravity-fed showerhead and provided just the right exotic atmosphere for my introduction to missionary life. I closed my eyes as cool water trickled through my dusty hair and splashed around even dustier feet. That's when I heard it. The all-too-familiar buzz.

My mind flashed back to the year before when Dan and I had made our first trip to this village. Mary, my local ministry partner, and I had been trying to make soap from wood ash and rendered beef tallow. It was my turn to stir the pot while Mary helped the other women with dinner preparations, so I was alone when the attack began.

First, there was one, then another, and another. Within seconds, bees swarmed my head and arms. I remember running toward the center of the hospital compound where my friends should have been gathering for the evening meal, but no one was there.

Enduring ungratefulness isn't pleasant, but it can lead to a surprising amount of contentment.

Before going to the mission field, we were required to attend safety and security training. Nothing covered what to do if attacked by African killer bees. But I had remembered a scene from a Winnie the Pooh cartoon in which bees chased Pooh, and he sought shelter in a pond. So I, too, had run to the only water source I could think of—the very shower in which I now stood.

I already knew from my first experience that the volume of water in the shower didn't dissuade bees. I remembered I thought I would die in this shower. But I didn't. A staff member from the hospital rescued me, and a team of ladies spent hours removing the stingers. What would happen now if I suffered another massive dose of bee venom?

The buzz grew louder. One bee entered the shower, then another, and another. My heart pounded and my head and ears felt hot and heavy. But this time, they weren't attacking. More bees came, but they still didn't attack. They just landed on my naked body and drank the beading water from my skin.

I wanted to run and scream, to streak across the compound to the shelter of my room. But modesty won out. Without even drying off, I threw my dress over my head and prepared for a hasty exit. "Ouch!" I must have trapped a bee! My eyes burned and vision blurred as I ran from the shower.

Questioning Gratitude

Some of the hospital staff saw my frantic state and laughed. "Teresa, you know you cannot shower in the middle of the day." Their taunting

followed me as I closed the door of my room and cried out, "God! How can I serve these ungrateful people? I've made a fool of myself in front of everyone. Maybe this isn't the place we should serve. And how can I live with these bees?"

Though I've never heard the audible voice of God, his answer resonated in my mind—loud and clear. "You are not here to serve these people. You are here to serve me."

What a wake-up call. When did I become so entitled, thinking I deserve gratitude? It's easy to get caught up in the altruism of Christian service and expect people to be grateful for our sacrifice. Some people are grateful, and it certainly feels good to be appreciated. But that shouldn't be what fuels our actions. Serving those who are unable or unwilling to give thanks brings unexpected, though often delayed, blessing and freedom.

Celebrating a Legacy of Service

Moses is a fitting role model for un-thanked servants. He freed millions of people from generational slavery, but did people say thank you? Certainly not. Instead, they spent the next several decades complaining, rebelling, and threatening mutiny and murder.[9] And what did Moses do? He took it to God—all of it: fears, failures, and frustrations.

Jesus also dealt with people who got too big for their britches. In Luke 10, seventy-two disciples returned after ministering in the surrounding towns. They told Jesus about their amazing work—expecting to get a pat on the back. But Jesus reminded them that he is the source of their power and authority.

When we recognize God as the one we serve and also as the source of the power behind our service, we can minister freely without worrying about what happens next. If people don't seem appreciative, that's okay. If the results don't look like what we expected—that's okay too.

---

9. Exodus 14, 15, 16, 17, 32 and Numbers 11, 14, 16, 20, 21

The work is the Lord's, and the glory is his as well. Our role is simply to do the work placed before us.

Enduring ungratefulness may not be pleasant, but it can lead to a surprising amount of freedom and contentment. As Paul said, *I have learned the secret of living in every situation, whether it is with a full stomach or empty, with plenty or little. For I can do everything through Christ, who gives me strength* (Philippians 4:12–13 NLT).

Being Free to Serve

God's voice comes back to me regularly. Not only as I serve on the mission field but also in everyday interactions when I'm in my American culture. Knowing I serve God enables me to make decisions on a different level. I don't need to think about meeting people's expectations or making them happy. I'm able to consider the purpose for which God has brought that person into my life and how God is glorified through our interaction.

Of course, no one can be gracious all the time. I remember traveling to a remote village by airplane. When I deplaned, authorities singled me out and took me to the back room of the two-room airport terminal. They searched my bags and flipped through my passport. "Why are you only searching *my* bags?" I said indignantly. Without a response, the man finished and waved me on.

Upon leaving the village, the same process occurred. "Why do you only search *my* bags when there are many other people?" I asked again.

"It's the job."

Discussing my encounter with friends, I later learned that his job is to conduct a security screening for foreigners. In my ignorance of the system, I likely came across as arrogant and unfriendly. The next time I went to that village, I greeted the man cheerfully and let him do his job.

Because I know the one I serve, I can do the right thing, even when others choose not to. I can endure being detained by airport authorities and stopped by traffic police for no apparent reason. When people are pushy or discourteous, I can give a smile in return because it isn't about how they treat me. It's about my Lord, whom I represent when I interact with them. I've learned that not expecting a thank you makes the gratitude I do receive all the sweeter.

A Cockatoo's Alarm

by Carin LeRoy

*C*HURCH SERVICES RARELY went without drama, and this Sunday was no different. A screaming baby, a dog wandering in, or an ear-deafening tropical downpour were the most common distractions. However, this time we had a new drama to deal with—a cockatoo.

After the singing finished, a white parrot (also known as a cockatoo) flew in to sit in the window opening where all the ladies and children sat. I could see him clearly—only ten feet ahead of me. At first, he sat quiet, looking around. Then he bounced by throwing his head forward, extending his yellow crest, and began to shriek. Loudly. His commotion interrupted the message.

Someone shooed him away.

We had been missionaries for years living among a small remote tribe in Papua New Guinea to share God's love with the people who lived here. In our earliest days, it was a challenge. We encountered cultural and language barriers, new foods, and rustic living. Yet, we learned to make necessary adjustments to raise a family and live among our tribal friends. There was never a dull moment.

A Sulfur-Crested Cockatoo

Before long, the cockatoo returned to sit in the same spot. It wasn't long until his agitation got the best of him, and he started another dance. His loud screeches paused the church service as everyone looked over at his disruptive behavior.

"He's angry and crying for food because he wants to eat," my friend said. I learned he belonged to a family in the village as a pet. After a while, he dozed off to wait for his human parent. I thought he was adorable. Where else in the world could you enjoy such a display?

We often saw the birds of the area, especially the long-beaked Papuan hornbill and the Sulfur-crested cockatoo. Papua New Guinea is known for its exquisite birds–of–paradise, but most stayed hidden in the jungle around us. However, these two birds were sometimes kept as pets in the village if caught at a young age.

One bird was black, and the other white, and their personalities were as different as their opposing colors. The black hornbill was a relaxed bird, content to hang around and watch. But the cockatoo's flamboyant personality made his presence known through his loud and obnoxious behavior. The large snow-white parrot was beautiful with a gray beak and feet. A cluster of yellow feathers on top of its head extended and fanned out when it felt excitement or agitation.

The local word for this parrot, *Ulo*, is the same word they use for the color white.

Cockatoos lived in the trees across the river from our house. Early in the mornings, we heard their screeches as they flew around, enjoying the sunrise after their night of sleep.

Don't doze on a limb and ignore the voice of a loved one who sounds an alarm.

The Family Commotion

One afternoon, as many people hung around our house, we heard the shrieks and squeals of a family of cockatoos down at the bend of the river. We looked over to see them flying around the top of the tree where they had been perched. In a panic, they were disturbed about something.

Neither my husband, Dale, nor I had any clue what was happening, but the local men immediately knew the meaning of the parrots' behavior.

"They see a snake and are afraid," one of the men said.

A snake in search of a meal wanted a cockatoo for dinner, and he was slithering toward the tree while they slept. The awake cockatoos flew around, using their panicked squawking to warn the others.

"Let's go find the snake," the men said.

The men left in the direction of the birds. Finding a big snake meant dinner for the village. About an hour later, they returned to show us their prize. A young man carried the dead reptile wrapped around his neck for us to see—a thirteen-foot python. That evening, the village cooking fires had roasted meat on the menu. They never wasted an opportunity to hunt for food. Most days, meals consisted of starches and vegetables, so fresh protein was an added treat for their evening spread.

A Prudent Warning

Families are important, even a family of cockatoos. When one bird sensed a killer snake, its cry of panic alerted every bird that danger was near. That evening, no cockatoo died. Their warning served a useful purpose for those who weren't aware that peril was close. If one cockatoo had ignored the panic and kept dozing on his limb, he would have been in the python's belly for dinner.

Just as the cockatoo alert and protect each other, our families and friends do the same for us. If they think something harmful is in our

lives, they will raise their concerns. Do we listen to their warnings? We often choose to ignore them and barge ahead in life. In Scripture, we read, *A wise man will hear and increase learning, And a man of understanding will attain wise counsel* (Proverbs 1:5 NKJV). A wise person considers the valid counsel of others.

The Concern of Others

When we've made a mess of things, we will often look back and see that someone close to us had raised their concerns. We can ignore others, or we can consider if their warning is legitimate. Perhaps they expressed worry about one of life's most important decisions: a marriage partner, hurtful patterns or habits, financial choices, or any other critical life choice.

God can and does speak through our family and friends. We need to consider a warning when it comes from those who know us best and love us most. Ignoring and moving forward without examination may lend itself to future heartache.

Let's live and learn well. When we contemplate the voiced concerns from our loved ones, consider what they see from their vantage. The more we adhere to the wise counsel of others, the better we can learn to navigate the challenges we face. Our choices are often wisest after we pray and seek advice. God often uses the loving voices of others to help lead us down a better path.

Don't doze on a limb and ignore the voice of a loved one who sounds an alarm.

I Can Hear You

by Lisa-Anne Wooldridge

*T*HE TWINKLING STARS overhead pulsed with color and light as I lay on the grass that clear summer night. The neighbor's dog burrowed into my jacket, his company warming me within and without. Restless, I'd shimmied my way out of my bedroom window for some quiet. Country girls know the secret. On some nights, the stars are like grape clusters of diamonds on a black velvet sky, and distant galaxies seem close enough to touch if you stare at them long enough. I was of an age to not expect an answer, but I still whispered to the sky, "Is anyone out there?"

Endless Connection

The golden retriever glued to my side raised and tilted his head and started wagging his tail as if someone he liked were approaching. I started to sit up when a sudden gust of wind blew across me and rustled loudly through the surrounding trees. The dog barked joyfully, and gooseflesh crept up my arms. Was I alone? I asked my question a little more loudly. "Is anyone out there?" But this time, I directed it to

53

the trees flanking my exposed hillside. Then, I heard it—what some people call a still small voice. But this was more like a text message in my mind. *I never leave you.*

My eyes widened as a tremor went through me. I lay back down, resting on the grass. How was this possible? I was eager to hear if the voice would say anything else, but nothing came. I relaxed and watched the sky until the galaxies started to dance, and I fell upward to land among them, lost in a dream where the stars seemed to sing.

I woke up in the grass the next morning, filled with wonder. I'd hurried back to my window before anyone found me out. Little did I know that my parents were aware of what I used to do all along: read under the blanket with a flashlight,

When I trust that voice, all my paths are peace.

give half my lunch away every day to the boy I liked, sneak out of my bedroom window to enjoy the summer nights, and so much more. I didn't get away with nearly as much as I thought I did.

Internal Alarm

Many years later, I've learned to trust that internal messaging system, whether it comes in the form of a mental text, gut feeling, or an inner voice. Once, as I was window shopping, a flock of birds went wild, singing above the shop next to me. I heard the voice, *Go see!* At the same time, my fiancé pulled my arm, saying, "Can you hear that?"

I immediately stepped backward, and just as I did, an elderly woman in an old Cadillac missed her brake, hit the gas, jumped the curb, and sailed straight through the plate glass window where I'd been standing one second before. The jacket I'd been admiring in the

window was pinned to the back wall. A pastor's wife standing across the square watched the whole thing. She insisted no birds were there at all, let alone the whole flock I'd heard.

Another time, I left my job on a lunch break to race home. I wanted to unplug my husband's computer and close the windows before a big storm hit. I needed to cross over a river on a large bridge to get there, but as I approached it, I clearly heard, *Go back.* I wavered, torn between my desire to take care of matters and to listen to that now familiar voice.

I turned around, and as I did, the sky turned green, and the wind picked up my little Rabbit truck with me in it. It gently scooped it off the road and set it down on the verge. I sped out of there and later learned that at the same time, a destructive tornado had struck the other side of the bridge, damaging it. I would have been on it. Thankfully, I listened to that urging rather than my common sense. Over the years, that quiet guidance protected me many times. It has always worked in my favor when I've faithfully followed it.

Power to Do More

Most of the time, the messages I received weren't dramatic or miraculous. They were often little things, gentle nudges to do something that turned out to be just what someone needed. At college, I once felt a nudge to send a tiny bit of leftover money at the end of the month to a friend who had already graduated. I mailed the ten dollars to him without explanation.

A month later, he replied. My ten dollars came just in time to buy gas for his empty tank. He needed it to get to his new job, or he'd lose it. If he lost the job, he'd lose his apartment within the month. This tiny gift gave him enough gas for the whole week before his first check. He even had enough to drive to an event center in his town where Billy Graham was speaking. My friend was a volunteer counselor and had

the joy of praying with two young people there who wanted to know more about Jesus.

He told me it was the best ten dollars of his life and marveled at how God must have given me the idea to share the little I had. I think it was the best ten dollars of my life, too, because it meant I could truly trust that voice.

Always On and Always Connected

I can often easily follow that voice and trust my internal messaging system with minimal faith. Ask that lonely-looking gal to lunch? No problem. Hello new BFF! Marry that tall guy who looks like a cross between Tom Selleck and Robbie Benson? Yes, Lord!

Occasionally, being obedient to that voice is more like taking a leap of faith—over a yawning chasm without a running start. Move across the country in the middle of a semester of grad school without a job or even a car? Oookay. Leave the community where you've put down roots for a quarter of a century after looking for, finding, and putting an offer on a house in a single weekend? Why not? I've learned that I can fully trust God's direction, no matter how scary or odd it seems. When I trust that voice, all my paths are peace.

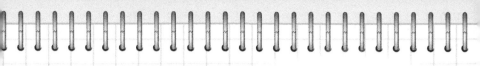

Can You See How Big I Am?

by Joanie Shawhan

I AM NOT A puny God.

I paused as these words reverberated in my spirit. The word *puny* isn't a part of my vocabulary. Was God speaking to me? I thought I believed God was mighty and all-powerful. But these words challenged me. Had I so underestimated the majesty and grandeur of God?

I reflected on the times I'd marveled at God's greatness. When staring wide-eyed out train windows as we clacked along tracks hugging ragged cliffs that plunged into deep gorges. Or as waves crashed against rocks while I stood on the shore contemplating how the waters ebbed back to sea, as if knowing their boundaries. The time Niagara Falls captivated me with its controlled power as whitewater cascaded over its horseshoe-shaped ledge and crashed into the river below.

I thought I'd been awed by the wonders of God. Maybe I needed a wider lens to appreciate his grandeur. How could I change my perspective? *I will meditate on the glorious splendor of Your majesty, And on Your wondrous works* (Psalm 145:5 NKJV). If I followed this instruction, would I experience the promised revelation of his majesty?

> *In the vastness and beauty of his creation, he unveils his majesty.*

Little did I know God had planned to fulfill this promise to me through an adventure that would once again open my eyes to his magnificence.

Bon Voyage

One day a friend dropped by with a brochure for an Alaskan cruise featuring one of our favorite Bible teachers. Would my roommate and I like to go? The trip sounded amazing, but how could I afford such an expensive vacation?

The hospital where I worked requested nurses to fill in extra weekend shifts, paying time and a half. Maybe picking up extra hours was the answer to my vacation fund. I was encouraged by the Scripture, *Whoever gathers little by little will increase it* (Proverbs 13:11 ESV). By faith, I placed a down payment on the cruise. I worked extra hours for the next six months until I had enough money to pay for my trip.

Our Alaskan adventure finally arrived. Tickets and passports in hand, we boarded the M.S. Westerdam at Port of Vancouver, British Columbia. We joined the other passengers laughing and chatting on deck as we jostled for positions at the rail awaiting our departure. Our excitement surged as the ship's horn bellowed and the vessel slowly pulled away from the dock. We entered the waters of the Inside Passage. Destination—Alaska.

We marveled at the feast God had prepared for us: the delicacies of fine dining, the beauty of nature, the teachings from his Word, and the sweetness of worship. Between scheduled meetings, we strolled the deck, inhaling the fresh, crisp air. Only the hum of the ship's engine interrupted this pristine environment. We glided through shimmering waters surrounded by miles of mountains seemingly untouched by man's hands yet carved by the hand of God.

Can you see how big I am?

Ports of Call

For our first port of call, we dropped anchor at the fishing village of Ketchikan. We boarded a seaplane, clinging to the metal rungs of the ladder as the plane pitched to and fro over the choppy waves. My heart raced in tandem with the motor as we sailed across the sea and lifted off into the Misty Fjords, a coastal rainforest formed by glacial and volcanic activity.

A double rainbow welcomed us, which I took as a sign of God's promise to me. I pressed my nose to the window, drinking in this breathtaking scenery, a picture painted by God. White mist clung to the snow-capped peaks like a fine smoke film. Waterfalls tumbled down cliffs into blue glacial lakes surrounded by lush foliage.

Can you see how big I am?

For one excursion, we boarded a bus in Juneau for the Mendenhall Glacier. This blue-tinged glacier zigzags 1500 miles and dates back to the Ice Age. For centuries, salmon dodged icebergs and navigated the whitewater, as if imprinted in their DNA, to reach their spawning ground near the glacier. I pondered the creative power of God, who had ordained such precise details.

As adventure continued, we boarded a catamaran for a four-hour cruise up the Lynn Canal to Skagway, a gold rush town. Trappers, traders, and fortune seekers traversed this glacial fjord for ages.

Not even one footprint escaped my notice.

As we settled into our canal cruise, I realized I didn't have any scheduled meetings or activities to attend. My task-oriented persona struggled to comprehend the peace and tranquility that enveloped me.

Rest in the beauty I created for your enjoyment.

I relaxed back in my seat and rested in the serenity of my surroundings. Multiple waterfalls cascaded down lush green mountainsides and splashed into the canal. Porpoises skimmed over our wake.

From Skagway, we boarded a six-passenger aircraft and flew over the ice caps of Juneau, which resembled fields of crackled glass. Streams

of water flowed down ragged cliffs and spilled into the rivers below. Between snow-capped mountain peaks, the setting sun glimmered in shades of gold.

Can you see how big I am?

Glacier Bay

On one tour, we entered Glacier Bay, gliding past the Margerie Glacier. Centuries of snow-packed ice—one hundred feet below the waterline and two hundred fifty feet high—spanned twenty-one miles. Every so often, a blue-tinged glacial chunk rumbled as it broke off and crashed into the water. Harbor seals sunned themselves on these remnants of calved icebergs scattered throughout the bay.

With binoculars poised on the brims of our noses, we scanned the horizon, searching for humpback whales. In the distance, we spotted several plumes of water spouting from their blowholes. Occasionally the whales breached. We clapped and squealed as they leaped, hauling their enormous bodies out of the water. Then their barnacled backsides smacked the water's surface in reverberating splashes.

Aren't my creatures delightful? Can you see how big I am?

Majestic God

God had challenged my understanding of his greatness when he impressed on my heart, *I am not a puny God.* In answer to my prayer, he beckoned me to join him on a journey into the wilderness of Alaska. While venturing into this pristine environment, he opened my eyes to his greatness and splendor in ways I never could have imagined.

Whether by whales, waterfalls, or foliage, God displayed his excellence in creation. The raw power of nature awed me and demonstrated the Almighty God in a mighty way. This same God transcends time and space. He has set the boundaries of every created thing, yet he knows no bounds. In the vastness and beauty of his creation, he unveils his majesty.

Now can you see how big I am?

Divine Connections

by Susanne Moore

*T*HE PHONE RANG, and a hesitant voice said, "You don't know me, but I need to talk to you." Since I was at work, I assumed she needed a quote for insurance. She meekly asked me, "Do you know Paul Haines*?" The back of my neck started to tingle. Tension pressed in as I stiffened and sat more alert.

Anxiety rose in my soul as I responded, "Yes, unfortunately, I do. Who are you? May I ask who gave my number to you?"

As she spoke, I thought, *Jesus, what are you up to?* The Savior and I have frequent conversations because I do not always choose well. Often, I question him about my circumstances. We communicate back and forth as I seek understanding. I'm grateful that he leads me to his truth. It is so good that his way is not my way!

But now, two years free from my abuser, a woman named Linda* called out of the blue asking me about him. I have discovered that Jesus faithfully draws women in who need to hear my story of joy and freedom. It leads all involved into a deeper relationship with him.

Through Commonalities

Linda said a woman I used to attend church with had given her my number. "I have been dating Paul for about six months regularly, and I really care for him. However, my children have had a tough time with him and want me to break it off."

Inside my head, I recounted the numerous conversations I had with my own children about the same thing. We shared a commonality in our stories. I boldly replied, "You are not going to like anything I have to say."

She whispered, "Well, tell me anyway."

Was I on *Candid Camera*? Was Paul sitting right there with her? My PTSD triggers were blowing up like firecrackers in my brain. Could I trust this person? I quickly pulled

God links souls together through story to strengthen our connection to the vine.

up Facebook on my cell phone, searched for our mutual friend, then the mutual friend's friend list, and found Linda. I saw her face. She looked older than me because of her solid gray hair. She seemed distinguished and strong. This reminded me that abusers choose victims based on their own depravity. As a survivor, I have learned that victims are not chosen based on their appearance, age, color, or size. I exhaled. "Please tell me your story first. How did you meet him?"

Through Differences

Relaxing slightly, I sat back in my office chair and listened. Linda's story began much like mine, yet vastly different. A chameleon morphs to the environment just like an abuser will know all about you before he even attempts to pursue you. He will adapt everything to your life and your loves, then reel you in by offering you all the things a woman's heart desires. I had learned it wasn't up to a man to supply my needs. It was up to God. *And my God will supply every need of yours according to his riches in glory in Christ Jesus* (Philippians 4:19 ESV).

Linda had been married for thirty years when her husband died suddenly. That was not my story. Mine was filled with brokenness. However, I knew instantly how our abuser found her—the same way he found me. When I was vulnerable and weak, when my faith wavered and questioned, the Enemy knocked on my door.

This lovely lady is a phenomenal artist (she sent me her website link). She told tales of Paul taking her to art museums, fine dining, and traveling afar. When he was with me, we did none of those things. Were we talking about the same man?

As Linda detailed the struggle with family and her deep desire to rescue this guy, I knew this was one of those amazing God things. He was using my story to help others. *But really God, my abuser's other girlfriends? Do I have to go there?*

I felt his Spirit nudge my heart. *She needs to hear truth.*

Through Truth

My life was in direct contrast with hers. Linda was a woman who had been kept well. She told me her marriage was incredibly good. Her husband left her financially set when he passed. She enjoyed the finer things of life. I am not financially set. Traveling is expensive, so I stick to the states. I have only failed at romance, and fine dining is too rich for my simple old soul.

When I sit in the same space with someone seeking answers, I turn them toward Jesus. Through many events in my life, I have learned that Jesus is the answer to everything. Jesus is the one who changes hearts. Jesus is the one who rescues. Jesus is the one who led her to call me. God was teaching in this moment.

Gently I shared with her, "You are in the very beginning of a relationship. Paul is grooming you for later. Reality is hard. He is incapable of love if he can abuse, manipulate, and gaslight you." As I began to unfold details of my relationship with him, she caught her breath and grew quiet.

I ended that conversation by asking her to contact me again after she chose to fully break free and not return to their relationship. Until then, I would be praying for her and hoping she chose the hard road to truth.

Through Relationship

A couple of months later, I received a Facebook message. All she said was, "I broke up with him." My heart leaped for joy over my new friend, who took the courageous step of breaking free. Knowing how difficult this decision was, I suspected she might be grappling with unprocessed emotions. Jesus asked questions. Jesus used stories to build relationships with people. I questioned, "How are you doing?"

She replied, "I am struggling. Can we meet for coffee?"

We spent a couple of hours over coffee, seeking God's truth and uncovering lies. Our discussion led us to discover Paul had been seeing her before he and I had even broken up. Before we parted that day, we took a selfie. See what God was doing in our lives to connect hurting women?

How powerful! The Redeemer rescued our lives from the threshold and is now building a relationship between two people who are uniquely different but with shared experiences. With wisdom beyond my understanding, Jesus uses my testimony in unprecedented ways to lead people to him. Think about it. The recounting of my abuse on Facebook led to the orchestration of two hearts bonding over brokenness. Now I am ministering to my abuser's victim. *Wow.* Jesus is awesome.

Jesus Christ links souls with mine through common and uncommon struggles to create lifelong divine connections. Sharing our stories and listening to the stories of others draws each of us closer to him and strengthens our connection to the vine. How will your life point others to Jesus? Just wait and see!

* Name changed.

I Didn't Anticipate That!

by Terri A. Robinson

I SETTLED BACK IN my seat with an air of expectancy. We had prepared for this field trip by reading *The Very Hungry Caterpillar* a number of times, observing caterpillars and butterflies, producing our own mini-books, and creating individual egg carton caterpillars and clothespin butterflies. We'd even discussed appropriate behavior in large groups.

Thus far, this excursion was going very well. When I'd put out the call for volunteers, several parents signed up—what a blessing! The children were excited to ride the school bus, and no one had gotten sick. All my three- and four-year-olds were accounted for. I *almost* felt guilty for being paid to work that day. As the theater darkened, all eyes were on the stage. I'd seated two of my anxious students near familiar adults. Everyone focused as the spotlight directed our attention. Then the curtain opened.

More Questions than Answers

The Very Hungry Caterpillar Show came to life and lived up to our highest expectations. While we waited to board the bus, students laughed and

chatted about the performance, the costumes, and the songs. Several needed to use the restrooms—which, of course, reminded everyone else of their biological needs. While time-consuming, I reminded myself it was fortunate they recognized the need *before* an incident happened.

I reflected on the musical and congratulated myself on exposing my students to a theatrical performance that enhanced their literacy experiences. It appeared the adults enjoyed it as much as the children.

It had been some time since I checked my phone. My husband's latest text was there. "They are on the way to the hospital now." *Who* was headed to the hospital? I scrolled to the earlier message. "It's on the prayer chain." *What* was on the prayer chain? I noticed two missed calls from my daughter.

I phoned my daughter first, surmising she was involved in this emergency, and confident that if she wasn't she would still be able to give me details.

"Mom, I'll have to call you back."

I then called my husband, who told me our precious, year-old grand-daughter had a seizure. The ambulance took her to the hospital. He wasn't sure where she was when this happened, if our daughter had followed by car, or if she was with her in the ambulance.

> The needs I anticipated were being met by the God of the universe before I even knew them.

Pray and Wait

Regardless of this personal emergency, I was still responsible for thirty-four preschoolers and attempted to remain calm and patient with those in my immediate care. The parents who went on the field trip took their own children home, and I set up the rest with some fun activities with markers or clay as I waited for an update from our daughter.

In the meantime, I was praying. Praying for our granddaughter.

Praying for my daughter. Praying for the doctors and any medical personnel working with her, for a correct diagnosis. I felt a curious mix of helplessness and peace. I fretted because they lived a few hours away, and I wanted to do something to lessen the burden. I was bolstered by the knowledge that others were praying before I even knew what happened.

Parents began arriving to sign out their children and take them home. This process often took about a half hour due to traffic around the building. I'm sure if anyone observed me closely, they would have noticed my smile was strained as I kept an ear tuned to the phone.

Finally, I got a call from our daughter. "I had to talk to the doctor. She had a high fever, which is now coming down. She has a mild case of pneumonia, and they are running tests to see if there's anything else going on. At this point, they think the seizure is from the fever. That's all."

Answers

She listened to my questions. She was remarkably calm. Yes, she had her car and expected to be home that evening. And no, our granddaughter wouldn't have to stay in the hospital.

Within an hour, our beautiful granddaughter was discharged. The doctors were almost certain the seizure was due to the high fever. She was given a prescription for antibiotics and instructions for her care. They appeared ready to snuggle at home for a few days before getting back into their routine. Already, she wanted something to eat.

The doctors were reassuring. My daughter was relieved that our granddaughter wanted food—a promising sign of being on the mend!

Reflections

As I drove home that afternoon, I reflected on what took place. What appeared to be a beautiful day turned into a time of tension after just reading one text! That led me to several rabbit trails of thought.

First, so many things happened that I was unaware of. Our

granddaughter was sick, and we didn't know the severity of it until she exhibited the seizure. How many times are there things going on behind the scenes that I am unaware of in my own life and in the lives of my family and students—until a more serious incident happens? Had I remembered to pray for each child's protection that morning? I couldn't remember, but I certainly would tomorrow!

Second, life goes on, whether I'm involved or not. I wasn't with my daughter, but God provided others to help take care of her needs, physically and spiritually. The doctors were there, and people were praying for our granddaughter before I even knew about it. Again, I was so very grateful for the believers who surrounded us.

Third—and this is the most precious of all—God himself was taking care of the situation even before I prayed. When I prayed for a correct diagnosis, tests were already being done. When I prayed for our daughter's peace of mind, my husband had already spoken words of reassurance, and she knew others were praying for her. The needs I anticipated were being met by the God of the universe before I even knew them.

∾

Tonight, our granddaughter took the stage. As the audience settled themselves, I reflected back to that field trip day when a stage was also in the spotlight. That day delivered a big dose of worry. What would become of my granddaughter? What a contrast. Tonight, as she danced, she was a shining reminder of God's loving attention to our needs, even before we ask.

Roots Run Deep

by Mary Harker

*M*ARY, THIS ISN'T *about you.* I heard God's voice speaking these words to my heart while taking a walk one morning. It was early in the pandemic with no foreseeable end. I was ready for the shelter-in-place mandate to be done, but the news kept getting worse. Praying while I walked, I asked God to end this plague that had taken over our lives, here at home and worldwide.

At first, I felt indignation at God's response to my request. *I know it's not about me, Lord, but this is so hard. Not just for me but for so many people.* However, during those morning moments, I understood God was working for *all* good in the middle of the mess. He works whether or not we see or feel him and doesn't waste any trial we face. We can not only survive the challenges that come our way, but we can thrive. Four lessons helped me stay strong and prevail in those early days of the pandemic.

God Is Strong in the Dark Places

When I can't see God working, I have two options. I learn to trust, or my faith flounders. My hope and dependence on God do not grow in

> *One move forward at a time keeps your mindset from spiraling out of control.*

times of ease and plenty. Times of darkness draw me to my knees and to the heart of my Father. Keeping my focus on Jesus helps me remain rooted during uncertainty and discouragement. When gale-force winds buffet a tree or there is insufficient water supply, it's in danger without firm roots. It would easily topple over and die. However, when a tree goes through wild storms and drought, the tree becomes sturdier as the roots grow deeper.

When I am firmly attached to God, I remain steadfast through the tempests that come my way. The fruit of the Spirit grows in my life when I am connected to him.[10] I stand on a solid foundation against the storms when Christ is my rock.

During the shutdown of the pandemic, God was moving. I read encouraging reports of people online hearing the gospel for the first time. Many ministries desired to be a place of encouragement and hope during this challenging season, and God blessed their creativity. People connected through online church services and Bible studies, Zoom meetings, Facebook Live, and virtual conferences or concerts. Those connections helped lighten the load for weary hearts and grow roots of faith to withstand the storms.

God Grows Unseen Fruit

I also came to understand that spiritual fruit grows below the surface before it's visible. Like the buried seed, rebirth is happening when we can't see growth. Jesus said, *unless a kernel of wheat is planted in the soil and dies, it remains alone. But its death will produce many new kernels—a plentiful harvest of new lives. Those who love their life in this world will lose it. Those who care nothing for their life in this world will*

---

10. John 15:4

70

keep it for eternity (John 12:24–25 NLT). God produces everlasting fruit in the dark and cold soil of hard times.

Dying to ourselves is never easy but worth the results. When we give up our comforts, plans, and desires, we gain the opportunity for God to bless us with abundance beyond what we can imagine. Not necessarily with physical generosity but with spiritual plenty.

Jesus came that we would have life abundantly.[11] When we are obedient and follow his voice, we receive his bounty. When we go through trials, God is glorified as we are purified.[12] Learning trust and submission gives me a deeper understanding of God's heart. And his compassion illuminates the darkness.

God Shines Brightest in the Night

Times of trouble radiate God's heart of love and compassion. His goodness and character shine strongest in the barren seasons, like the smallest beam that illuminates the darkness. We don't always understand his ways, and sometimes we may not hear his voice. Yet he promises to always be with us and never leave us.[13]

Scripture is full of illustrations of his promise. When Moses was in the desert, he experienced the burning bush. The Israelites followed the pillar of fire in the wilderness. Elijah saw the fire of God burn the sacrifice placed on the altar when confronting the prophets of Baal. After coming through hardship, like Job, I can say my eyes have seen God.[14] When I come to the end of myself, I reach out and cling to the God who proves himself faithful.

When I go through a dark season and draw near to God, I experience his tender loving care. He reminds me of his protection through various methods: his Word, a message I hear, or encouragement from a friend. These sweet communications provide the strength I need to keep moving forward.

---

11. John 10:10
12. 1 Peter 1:7
13. Matthew 28:20
14. Job 42:5

God Points a Way through the Wilderness

Not only does God give the light for our path, but he gives us the way through the wilderness. *Your word is a lamp to guide my feet and a light for my path* (Psalm 119:105 NLT). When the course is long and hard, he goes before us and shows us the next step. Usually, he does not reveal the whole journey at once.

As we move forward one step at a time, we keep the momentum to forge ahead. It's more challenging to move a stationary object than one that continues to propel forward. And like the Israelites in the desert, we receive daily manna or bread. God usually only gives us enough to make the next move.

It was easy for me to drift day by day during the pandemic. The isolation and feeling of purposelessness led to feelings of depression and hopelessness. I realized I needed to break this cycle. I started a daily schedule, took long walks around our neighborhood, and listened to weekly Quarantine Quiet Time! by Matthew West on Facebook.[15] The daily schedule added purpose to my day. While walking, I prayed and talked with my neighbors, which improved my feelings of isolation. The positivity I heard weekly from Matthew and his team gave me a brighter outlook. One move forward at a time kept my mindset from spiraling out of control.

Trials often leave us feeling overwhelmed and even overlooked by God. We try only to get by. However, we don't need just to endure. Instead, we can use those times to grow deep roots. There is abundant growth beyond what is visible. We see God shine his brightest in the dark and point a way through the wilderness.

Friend, God is always with us, and he is always working on our behalf. On my walk early in the pandemic that day, God impressed on my heart that it wasn't all about me. He reminded me *all* things work for good.[16]

---

15. Matthew West, Quarantine Quiet Time!, Facebook, multiple dates, https://www.facebook.com/matthewwest.
16. Romans 8:28

Stinky or Sweet

by Robin Steinweg

N O ONE SEES our thoughts. Yet they are the birthplace of our words. And our words have the power of death and life.[17] Doesn't it make sense, then, to foster the sweetest-smelling thoughts?

I entered this world with a negative default setting. Even though I'm a bonafide glass-half-full optimist, stinkin' thinkin' takes up residence and erects a whole infrastructure hidden behind my smiling face.

It's impossible to count the ways our thoughts can take a stinky turn. Let me share a few I've battled, along with their antidotes.

Insecurity

Threads of insecurity began to weave through my life when I was a young child.

"Hi, Ugly." "Hey, Knobby-Knees Nelson, are those your knees, or are you smuggling out nuts?" "Hi, Stick-Girl." I dreaded the game Red Rover. A line of kids held hands, and someone from the opposite

---

17. Proverbs 18:21

team was commanded to break through. I bounced backward with fist bruises on my tummy, laughter burning my ears. I believed the taunts. Even as an adult, I find it uncomfortable to wear knee-exposing shorts.

One thing unravels my insecurity: learning how God sees me and speaking his words to silence harmful voices. *I am the apple of God's eye.*[18] *I am wonderfully made.*[19]

Failure

Failure at anything domestic used to define me. In my life skills class, I sewed a pair of shorts. Yeah, *shorts* (a teacher-chosen project). I might've tried harder had the pattern been for a floor-length skirt. But to make something that would show my legs? No, thanks. When I tried them on, they fell apart. Obviously, I had no aptitude for sewing.

Our thoughts are the birthplace of our words.

Later, a couple of newlywed culinary disasters convinced me I was hopeless in the kitchen. I made fun of myself before anyone else could. I boasted what a rotten cook I was, defeating my attempts before I even opened a cookbook. Can't sew, can't cook, must be terrible at anything housewifely. Those thoughts spread like yeast through dough. They rose to negate all my attempts at managing a home.

This example of how stinking thoughts and words bring death certainly killed my desire to keep the house. Years later, after hearing a message about the power of words, I determined to speak the opposite. I'd snort and laugh as I said, "I'm a good cook." Untrue! But I spoke in faith that God could change me. Within a year, I had a list of meals I was good at, and people asked for the recipes. I began to think of myself as a good cook. God loves our faith!

---

18. Psalm 17:8
19. Psalm 139:13–14

Self-Righteousness

The reek of self-righteousness took root in high school. I thought I was compassionate, loving, and the defender of underdogs. But my best friend became anorexic. I witnessed cruel and mocking words hurled at her by the popular crowd. I equated snobbery and hateful behavior with popularity. I judged anyone who was friendly with the mockers, though I didn't know them, their histories, or their hearts. I despised them.

What changed for me? Jesus. The Bible convicted me of my unworthiness and sin. I deserved judgment. Even my good deeds were like filthy rags compared with God's goodness.[20] But God didn't leave me there in my sin. He helped me understand that Jesus took unjust punishment for my sins. He did this because of his limitless love. One perfect sacrifice for all, forever. When I received this truth, he changed my heart. He's still changing my heart as I allow him to live through me.

Complaining

I've often joked about complaining. "I've got funny ears," I used to tell my sons. "They don't hear whining." I have a low tolerance for it. Yet I do my share. *It's too cold. It's too windy. I'm too hot. I'm tired of . . .* whatever! God does not smile when I grumble.

A few years back, spring break approaching, my students anticipated trips to warm climates. I felt happy for them until they asked where I was going. They looked disappointed or pained at hearing I'd have a productive work week. I experienced thoughts that came from a very warm place indeed. Satan lost no time helping me plan a weeklong pity party! But God reminded me that my need to organize my home that week was because he'd blessed us with books, students to bolster our income, and papers from the privilege of home-educating our sons.

---

20. Isaiah 64:6

He showed me that dirty dishes mean we have food. Dirty laundry means we have clothes. Thankfulness crowded out self-pity. The sunlight streaming in even appeared brighter. Gratitude—the attitude to lift a mood!

Fear

Some years ago, my doctor told me I had a cyst, and tests indicated a possibility of ovarian cancer. I'd need surgery. Soon.

At the time, I didn't know anyone who had survived this diagnosis. Fear caused shallow breathing, tight throat, gnawing stomach, and a pounding heart. I'd startle awake wondering who would raise my sons and be there for my husband. I grieved for my parents losing a daughter so young.

But God's Spirit knocked gently, persistently. *Do not fear.* Do you know that the Bible tells us not to fear hundreds of times? I'd learned that even one repetition means to pay extra attention. This number meant serious business. It meant obedience. I'm not gonna lie; it was a battle. Fear screamed. God's Word whispered. I had to fight to hear him. It took energy, prayer, and renewing my mind with God's Word before I could bring fear-thoughts into captivity. By the time I'd had the ovary removed and waited for the oncology report that told us there was no cancer, I'd begun a good habit of overcoming fear by listening to God.

Comparison

Do all of us compare ourselves with others? It's a common pitfall.

Recently I joined a gym. A trainer helped me with machine settings so I wouldn't irritate old accident injuries. On one machine, the person before me had used 150 pounds. My setting? Zero. Zip. *I'm a wimp!* Worse, I could barely work the machine. *Noodle arms.* Resting, I noticed other exercisers working, lifting, running, and sweating. I brushed the sweat from my forehead. Sweat! In a beat, I realized that

my body was working as hard at zero pounds as the person ahead of me had at 150 pounds. I apologized to the Lord for comparing and accepted the approval I sensed from him. As always, he'd provided the answer.

Thoughts can't be seen but have power for death or life. God's words are the aroma of life. We can choose to train our thoughts. Will they be stinky—or sweet?

Stretched Too Thin

by Diana Leagh Matthews

*B*ONE WEARINESS WASHED over me. "It's Thursday," I muttered, struggling to move to a sitting position. For years, my body told me when it was Thursday because I was so tired it was all I could do to get up and make it to work. I had a love/hate relationship with my job. I loved those I served and the work but hated the long hours, physical toil, and unrealistic requirements.

"What's the answer, Lord?" My soul screamed. I didn't have time to look for another job. Not while working ten- to twelve-hour days, studying for a work-related intensive class, and struggling to meet publishing deadlines. I'd stretched myself too thin and had been doing so for years. My body creaked with arthritis, ached from weariness, and struggled to push through.

I reflected back to when I started this job seven years earlier. After being unappreciated in my previous position, I felt I had something to prove.

"Don't take on too much. You'll regret it because it will become expected of you," my mentor reminded me often.

However, I couldn't give less than my best. Over time, that best became a noose around my neck. My life revolved around work and the residents in the nursing home.

My workdays comprised pushing wheelchairs, teaching various classes, planning parties, attending meetings, entering paperwork into the computer, implementing fundraising ideas, and decorating for that month's holiday. Not to mention numerous other tasks thrown my way.

While I wanted to think I was wonder woman, I wasn't. I couldn't do it all and had to learn how to ask for help and delegate to my staff.

Stay focused on balance to prevent being stretched too thin.

Learning Self-Honesty

I became lonely in my drive to serve others. The loneliness screamed at me, and I struggled to find other ways to meet people outside of work. I attended Sunday church services, but long hours made further involvement difficult. I had joined several writing groups, a theater group, and an online weight-loss group—all of which I loved. However, it stretched me too thin. I'd get home at seven o'clock or later, attend an online meeting or have a rehearsal for two hours. At least once a week, there were still responsibilities to tend to before I could go to bed. I cooked for fundraisers, prepped crafts for activities, and researched future projects.

Eventually, I had to drop half the groups. There was no way I could keep up the pace. However, loneliness consumed me regularly.

Then a pandemic hit, and my responsibilities increased. The residents needed me more than ever as we went on lockdown.

Lamenting Within

"God, help me." This became my daily cry as I experienced burnout and stress. "I don't know how much more I can take." Weariness consumed me.

The desire for change bubbled within me. I struggled to figure out what it might be.

Finally, I finished my classes and met my deadlines. However, the weariness refused to leave. Too many days, all I could do was lie on the couch after work, too exhausted to move.

I strived to eat healthy and exercise, and it helped to feel better, but it did not remove the fatigue.

Then people at work started to ask, "What's wrong with you? You don't smile like you used to."

"I'm tired," I'd tell them. *If only you knew how tired.* Depression became my constant companion, and restlessness replaced sleep.

Taking another job was the logical answer, but I wondered how I'd ever leave the residents. I worried about them. Would anyone else advocate for them the way I did? One day, I returned from vacation (still feeling unrested) to discover that instead of residents talking with me about specific needs, they had gone over my head. I waited a week for someone to speak with me, but no one did. The matter ate at me until I addressed the situation, and we ironed out the issues. However, during that time, something broke within me. I was done in a way I'd never been done before.

My heart continued to cry out to God. "I can't take this anymore. What do I do?" I felt like a failure. As if I were letting the residents down. The Lord reminded me that *my flesh and heart may fail, but God is the strength of my heart and my portion forever* (Psalm 73:26 ESV).

Each morning, I forced myself to go to work and make it through the day. It weighed heavily on my mind. I prayed and sought answers, but they did not come.

Seeking God

Within a week, I discovered we were under a corporate takeover, and my position was not retained. Half our department had been cut. Peace washed over me at the news. Relief flooded my soul.

The next weeks and months brought all the stages of grief (denial, bargaining, anger, depression, and acceptance), but the peace remained. The Lord provided for my needs.

In my weariness, I turned to the only person and place I knew to turn—to the Lord God. After all, Jesus told us, *Come to me, all who labor and are heavy laden, and I will give you rest . . . for I am gentle and lowly in heart, and you will find rest for your souls* (Matthew 11:28–30 ESV).

I set out on a journey of self-discovery. I had to figure out why I'd pushed myself so hard, what I wanted in life, and what type of job to search for. The answers did not come immediately. I underwent a lot of soul searching, prayer, and Bible study—pulling back the layers.

The first few months, I noticed I could only do a little, and then I needed to rest. I didn't fight it but gave myself permission to slow down.

Learning Self-Care

Eventually, I noticed I was taking better care of my health—eating better, more exercise, increased soul maintenance, and practicing better self-care.

Four months after my job ended, a little spark of life appeared in my soul. It felt weird after being depressed for so long. I picked up a book and read for enjoyment for the first time in years. I found other long-lost passions such as genealogy research, reaching out to friends, and day trips. Then I explored the town where I'd lived and visited various attractions. I'd never had a chance to check these places out before due to my work demands.

Six months have passed since my job ended, and it continues to be a journey. I've found a better balance and prioritized the need for soul-care and self-care. I'm taking time to rest and creating harmony between my commitments and writing life.

For me, it's a journey as I continue to practice personal steward-ship, like changing my eating and exercise habits. It's been a difficult lesson, but one I'll never forget. I know there's still a long way to go on this path.

As I prepare to start a new job, I remind myself to stay focused on balance to prevent being stretched too thin.

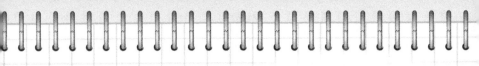

Redress My Naked Soul

by Susanne Moore

A WALL OF BLUE ocean water swallowed me whole and drew me back into the depths of the sea. I was tossed around like a rag doll—gasping for air, gulping water, and praying for landfall. With a final push, the undercurrent spat me out like a cannonball, fast and hard. The dense powder felt like concrete against my skin.

As I gathered my wits, I blew sand from my mouth and attempted to sit up. Shaking, I fell backward, catching myself with my hands. Life had pulled me into the undercurrent many times. I sure did not see it coming. What just happened? I felt weak. How did I get here?

Spontaneous Decisions

My tendency is to act before I think. Therefore, I find myself in situations I could have avoided. Have you ever thought, *That was a dumb move*? It's engraved in my mind from years of foolish actions. Swimming the butterfly in the ocean was a dream for this seasoned swimmer. Water—my go-to holiday. When I planned the trip to Oahu, I had no idea that this part of the island was covered in a shallow reef. I had

already sliced my knee on the jagged rock. You cannot do the butterfly in shallow rocky water. We had to find somewhere else to swim.

We wanted to experience Hawaii on this expensive vacation, not just visit. So, upon the advice from locals, my daughters, brother, sister-in-law, and I drove to the North Shore. We didn't know that their directions led to an unpredictable place. It's possible the locals were chuckling under their breath after we left, "Joke's on you, tourist."

I mean, we did go shark fishing at midnight for one hundred dollars each. Yes, I spent three hundred dollars to take my girls miles into murky waters in the middle of the night with strangers. It was not a very big boat!

> *A ten-minute moment became a pivotal undressing of my shame and redressing of my soul.*

Proceeding Anyway

At the North Shore, my daughters were excited to dive into the ocean. We walked out onto the beach. Young children rode surfboards. Families sprinkled the shoreline. A man threw a frisbee to his golden retriever. This was it! This is why we came here.

My sister-in-law spread out a blanket and started pulling out our sandwiches and chips for our picnic. My brother stood nearby with a video camera to showcase our adventure. We threw off our flip-flops and headed down to the water's edge.

We laughed, splashed each other, and dove into the waves as they came in. Wading in a little further, we turn around to wave at the camera. It was a magical moment for this proud mom. Pride is one of those protective walls I erect for safety and preservation. Pride is also the precursor before falling or flailing.

Raw Reality

My brother screamed, "Watch out!" Unfortunately, it was too late. I didn't have time to brace myself or anticipate what was going to happen. This served in my favor because I could have been hurt physically. But, alas, only my pride was wounded during the "tragic" accident.

As I sat there befuddled in the sand, the laughter again penetrated my ears, and I tried to look toward the sound.

My daughters were across the beach. One stood over the other, trying to help her up. The one on the ground held her knee. I noted the pain written on her face. *How did they get that far away from me?* That's when I discovered my brother down on one knee, laughing hysterically. The video camera was attached to his wrist but lay haphazardly in the sand.

What's going on? I moved my right hand over to the left side of my torso, trying to twist myself into a standing position. As I stood up on wobbly legs, I wrenched my body. I stretched my arms and shook out my limbs, trying to recover from the landing.

My sister-in-law tried to mouth something, but I couldn't understand her. My daughters came toward me, yelling, "Mom, look!" I gawked around me, thinking maybe another wave was about to snatch me up. The girls approached and spread their arms out wide together as if they were sheltering me. I was at a loss to know what was the matter. They simultaneously screamed, "Mom, you are naked!"

What? My swimsuit was not on my body.

I looked down and discovered my unvarnished frame in all its glory. Embarrassment crept up from my toes to my nose. I quickly prayed, "Lord Jesus, a cloud from above would be truly appreciated right now." I dropped and rolled—hoping it was quicksand.

Ladies, I'm a bold, blonde, heavy-set woman—mostly body positive when I'm dressed and have carefully covered up my imperfections. However, I happened to be the largest I had ever been in my life at that moment. I felt like a beached whale. Now that is the naked truth.

I was petrified and could not move. I just lay there—white sanding my shame. Could life get any more embarrassing? My brother was video-taping. He saw me *naked*! He told me he was "scarred for life!"

My family was not the only group laughing. I wanted to bury more than my body in that sand. Something had to give. I had a choice to sink or swim. Where was my swimsuit? Before someone found my swimsuit floating nearby, before I made a mad dash for the swimsuit and dove into the ocean naked, and before I struggled to put it on underwater, I had to choose to stand.

Covered by Grace

To be vulnerable is to be stripped naked of protective walls that I have erected for protection in a cruel world. In choosing a life in Christ, he beckons me to lay down my burdens, uncover the pain, remove the veil, and collapse at his feet. I was exposed at the feet of others. It took strength and courage to embrace myself bare and rise. A ten-minute moment became a pivotal undressing of my shame and redressing of my soul. It taught me the value of living vulnerably, being courageous, embracing my flaws and weaknesses, and coming out clothed in righteousness and dressed in grace.

In hindsight, I would not take my young teenagers shark fishing at night since that's when sharks feed. I would not take them to the North Shore because a fifty-foot wave could be much worse than being caught in the buff. I'm grateful that my daughters look at our family excursions as special days spent with Mom. I find joy in their laughter, remembering when Mom was thrown to shore in her birthday suit on a beach in Hawaii. The experience has inadvertently transformed my most embarrassing moment into a lifetime of living vulnerably and baring my soul to help others.

Secrets of the Quilt

by Nancy Kay Grace

Q UILTS INTRIGUE ME, as they represent the quilter's creativity through colors and patterns. I desired to make one when I was a young mom with two active children. Despite life's busy season, I chose to learn this new craft for some unknown reason. However, because my house didn't have room for large quilting frames, I searched for an alternative method. Someone in my church recommended an older lady named Florence, who taught lap-quilting in her home.

Lap-quilting allows for portability of the project without cumbersome frames. My simple desire to learn quilting the old-fashioned way taught me more about life than the art itself.

The Brave Beginning

I drove to Florence's old farmhouse in town with the instruction to enter by the back door and go downstairs. Stepping into her house, I descended the narrow, creaky staircase, turning sideways and ducking my head to go to the basement.

This haven of creativity featured a large wooden worktable in the

center of the well-lit room. Tables stacked with neat piles of fabric lined the walls. In every direction, wherever I looked, was an abundance of colorful calicos and solid colors of every hue.

Florence's gentle spirit greeted me as she smiled, introducing me to the other women in the small group. Eager to learn this new skill but also a bit timid, I took my place at the table. I felt nervous about using a thimble and quilt needle, although I was familiar with sewing.

I stuck the thimble on my finger, ready to begin. Florence demonstrated how to make small, even stitches. In an awkward attempt, I started basting together the edges of two small squares of blue calico. My quilt lesson had begun. That first day, I left feeling confident that I could learn this art.

My desire to learn quilting the old-fashioned way taught me more about life than the art itself.

At first, we made pillows. Learning to put colors together, choosing the quilt patterns, and getting the hang of different techniques helped my confidence grow. Week by week, Florence prepared us for a larger project.

Imagine my surprise when one month into the classes, Florence announced, "Now it's time to do a project." What I thought was the project was not the project. She meant a quilt, not pillows.

Tackling Harder Lessons

I realized my overblown ambition was greater than the confidence in my ability. Was I ready to tackle a large quilt?

My first thought was to make a full-sized quilt, but then I realized it would take me forever to finish. Next, I thought of making a twin-sized quilt, but I would have to make two: one for each of my children. Again, too big of a project for me. I settled on creating a four-square wall hanging, each square with a different pattern.

Straight seams appeared simple enough, but I still managed to

make mistakes. In each class, I had to take out stitches and redo the piecing. Every week, Florence patiently spoke in her quiet voice, "Just think of what you're learning by doing this."

Those words—which I heard frequently—did not comfort me.

My exasperation from ripping out seams overshadowed my enjoyment. Piecing together one quilt square took weeks. As a young woman, I felt pressure to get things done and move on to the next thing. I considered yielding to the temptation of using my sewing machine, skipping the hassle of hand-stitching.

I asked Florence, "How long does it take to finish a quilt?" She had handmade many quilts with ease.

Her calm reply? "As long as it takes."

Why did I think learning this art would be easy? I thought about giving up from discouragement and the pricked, sore fingertips more than once.

I had only finished three of the four squares when the class sessions ended. Now I was on my own to use my limited quilting knowledge. The project was too far along for me to throw it aside or make it into pillows. Sheer determination and grit motivated me to conquer the basic wall hanging. Florence graciously gave me permission to contact her if I needed guidance.

Patching Frayed Emotions

Months later, I arranged a time to return to Florence's farmhouse. I felt eager to receive her instructions for finishing my handmade quilted wall hanging. My preschool-aged daughter accompanied me.

Florence carefully showed me how to attach the borders, miter the corners, and trim the seams. After stitching the last border sash, I breathed a sigh of satisfaction. One final seam to trim, and my small quilt would be complete.

I started trimming that seam on the back of the project, but my daughter distracted me with an innocent question. Looking up to answer her, I took my eyes off my work. The blades of the scissors closed,

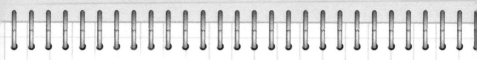

slashing the finished quilt top. My heart sank as I felt the color drain from my face. I wanted to cry. How could I do such a careless thing?

Noticing my despair, Florence placed her wrinkled hand over mine, patted my hand, and calmly spoke, "We can fix it. Just think of what you're learning by doing this."

I fought back tears in an attempt to patch my frayed emotions. Florence gently showed me how to repair the slash. She never criticized, only encouraged and instructed me.

The final mistake was not the end of the project. The quilt top was repaired, and the slash was hardly noticeable.

Perseverance paid off. The finished project—my masterpiece—finally hung on my wall.

Secrets of the Quilt

Looking at my small quilt with a sense of accomplishment, I see more than blue and brown calico stitched with hand-quilting. I learned more from Florence than choosing colors, patterns, and techniques.

The secrets of the quilt have stayed with me throughout life: patience and perseverance, gentleness of spirit, slowing down to allow the flow of creativity, determination to finish a long project, and letting God shape me.

Do the pieces of my life fit together into the design God desires for me? I only see the moment-by-moment piecing and, at times, feel overwhelmed by pressures and challenges. I think I have learned a life lesson but mess up again, needing the mending of the Holy Spirit. I feel the tug of every stitch in my life and sense the Lord saying, "Just think of what you're learning." God sees the finished project, a completed quilted masterpiece reflecting the nature of the Creator.

> *For we are His workmanship, created in Christ Jesus for good works, which God prepared beforehand that we should walk in them.* (Ephesians 2:10 NKJV)

When we yield the pieces of our lives to the Master Designer, the patchwork of our lives makes sense. Despite mistakes, we learn the secrets of living in God's grace.

True Treasures

by Joanie Shawhan

I LOVE TO-DO LISTS. A check mark by each task on my list validates my accomplishments.

As a nurse, my task-oriented nature served me well. Part of my responsibility included administering treatments and medications to my patients on time.

When I'm focused, I generally don't appreciate interruptions in my agenda. Then there is my friend Spanky. For Spanky, time is a set of numbers encircling a dial. I received quite a revelation regarding tasks and time when Spanky and I decided to take a Caribbean cruise together to celebrate her milestone birthday and my one-year cancer survivorship.

Travel Treasures

Spanky and I both love to shop and took full advantage of the ship's boutiques. When I shop, I select my items, pay, and leave. Not Spanky. After extended browsing, she chatted with the manager and drew out

the woman's life story before finally paying for her purchases. I stood nearby and tapped my foot while my eyes darted back and forth between Spanky and my watch. Despite my annoyance, I felt drawn into these impromptu conversations. I started to slow down and listen to their stories.

Spanky's congenial personality and genuine interest in people encourage even strangers to share snapshots of their lives with her. Through her conversations, we discovered one of the managers had worked with several cruise lines. She disclosed the pros and cons of each company as well as some of her favorite vacation spots. One of the clerks escaped her home in war-torn Bosnia by answering an employment ad for the cruise line.

I am changed for the better by the stories that have been woven into the fabric of my life.

We repeatedly bumped into two women from Canada who shared their favorite vacation adventures, including stories of all-inclusive resorts in Cuba. One day when I chatted with one of the Canadians, the woman announced she had just finished spending her fifteen-minute daily quota in the sun.

I'd later learn that while we had a superficial conversation, the other woman was confiding in Spanky that she had received a recent breast cancer diagnosis, a report she would share with her friend after the cruise.

As our trip drew to a close, I discovered that the people we shared stories with enriched our cruising experience. Sometimes I approach life like a horse on a racetrack wearing blinders, waiting for the gun's blast to start the race, focused on the finish line. As much as I like to

stay focused, I had never realized the joy I missed because I didn't allow God to interrupt my agenda.

Maybe the time had come for me to allow God to interrupt my routine and listen to the stories of others. Little did I know that God had a plan to retune my ear.

Survivor Treasures

When I was diagnosed with ovarian cancer, I sought out other survivors for encouragement and support. But I found none.

Several years later, I wrote *In Her Shoes: Dancing in the Shadow of Cancer* to help other women navigate the storms of cancer and chemotherapy. As I listened to the stories from the eleven other women included in the book, I experienced the validation I had sought through our shared chemotherapy experiences.

Despite the seriousness of cancer, I couldn't help but laugh at their stories about flying wigs, kissing pigs, and nightly serenades of toilet flushing—that one courtesy of a pet monkey. One woman shared about an overly friendly baby alligator stranded after a hurricane. With regularity, the alligator waddled across the golf course and butted his nose on the sliding glass door of the family home. The gal thrust a ration of crackers and cookies through a crack in the door, probably contributing to his eventual eight-foot bulk.

Their stories provided me an opportunity to walk, for a season, in their shoes.

Vintage Treasures

Marilyn, a woman I met at the pool, called me one day. "I'd like to purchase four more of your books, and would you like to come for lunch?"

I hesitated. A ticker tape of my pre-holiday to-do list scrolled through my mind.

"You don't have to come for lunch . . . " I heard the disappointment in her voice.

"I'd love to come."

As a retired swimming instructor, she had volunteered to help me with my backstroke. She won multiple blue ribbons for swimming in the senior Olympics in her age category and planned to swim in nationals shortly after her ninetieth birthday.

Marilyn greeted me in the entryway, surrounded by her collection of oriental art: a grandfather clock, a carved table, and a series of wall hangings. All were black lacquer inlaid with mother of pearl.

I not only feasted on lunch. The vintage collections dispersed throughout her home also provided a feast for my senses. How could I refuse a tour of her treasures when I saw how her eyes sparkled as she wound one music box after another?

After lunch, Marilyn led me to her grand piano and slipped a scroll into the spool box. Strains of "Hark! The Herald Angels Sing" filled the room. I learned the player piano had been discarded as junk, but an artisan restored and restrung the instrument. Marilyn and her husband had discovered this piano through their membership in the Musical Box Society International, which promotes the preservation of automated musical instruments. They were delighted to meet other music box enthusiasts. The organization provided them with opportunities to visit private collections, tour Europe, and travel the country attending various events.

Next, I followed her to a 1906 music box, another gem acquired via their Musical Box Society connections. She plugged a nickel into the slot and turned the crank. A Regina disc with punched holes dropped into the player and plucked the strains of a nineteenth-century tune. The music box reminded me of my uncle. On one of my visits, he had placed a silver disc in his phonograph-style music box. I stared at the comb as it swept over the punched holes, mesmerized by the instrument's clear tones.

In another room, a black carousel horse raised a white-socked hoof as if poised for battle. A crusader cross and a lion crest embellished

his cape. Marilyn said that during their travels with the Musical Box Society, one of the members had raved about a nearby carousel museum. Before heading home, Marilyn and her husband had decided to take a detour and check out the exhibit. Enamored by the workmanship of the full-sized carousel horses, her husband commissioned one for an anniversary gift.

Seeing the horse triggered memories that transported me back in time. How I had delighted in my first carousel ride, going around, my little hands clenching the gold bar, bobbing up and down to the rhythm of the calliope.

Marilyn's vintage collections spoke volumes to me about her life story.

True Treasures

These stories and many others have enriched my existence. I marvel at how others' testimonies inspired me and offered me courage in the face of adversity. Their wisdom and examples have guided me. Sometimes I've laughed. At other times I've wept. But I am changed for the better by the people whose stories have been woven into the fabric of my life.

They are magnificent gifts. True treasures.

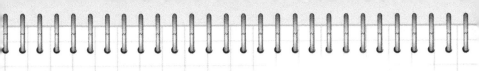

The Season for Love

by Edna Earney

*U*GH, THIS RAIN!" Irene moaned as we circled through the Hi-D-Ho turnaround on the strip.*

We cruised Polk Street in downtown Amarillo that spring evening, looking for friends, checking out guys, trying to drive the boredom from our usual dateless Friday night. Irene and I joked we would become the first Baptist nuns.

"Yep. April showers bring May flowers," I chirped.

"I still want to find Donnie. If he asked Susan out, they might be at Osage. Let's spy on them!"

Short-Lived Spies

Irene was twitterpated. Donnie was a senior drum major. Irene wanted him to notice her, a lowly sophomore flutist in the band. So far, the only attention she'd garnered was when Donnie warmed up the band at the beginning of practice, and he pointed the baton at Irene once to play middle C. She grooved off that mite for a month.

I aimed my '57 Chevy toward Osage Park—nothing but a parking

lot with a dozen spaces, nestled a hundred yards back from a dirt road at the edge of town. It was a favorite spot to "go parking" in 1970. Irene might never have a date with Donnie, but she was willing to torture herself by catching him kissing someone else.

As we left downtown, the spotty rain picked up. In the Texas Panhandle, frequent winds push the red clay dust onto the roads. When the clouds spit rain, it results in a snot-slick surface resembling a toddler's leaky nose. With the increasing rain, I slowed down on the muddy road to spot the unmarked turn into Osage Park. I spotted it ahead.

Reaching the lot, I turned off my headlights.

"I hate this rain!" Irene put her face to the window. "I can't see anything. You know Donnie's Dodge Charger. See it?" Then a car turned in, headlights glaring. Irene ducked—she surely didn't want to be caught spying. "What dimwit came in with their headlights on?" She mumbled against her knees.

"I don't know." I winced at headlights gleaming in the rearview mirror.

"Gun it!" Irene shouted. "It might be the cops! Whoever it is let everyone in the whole world see your car. Move!"

High-Centered Anxiety

I gassed it, gained ground, then let up as we reached the turn. Seeing no cars for miles, I ignored the stop sign and whipped onto the road. I felt the tires spin, the car slide. Panic. I saw the drainage ditch looming through the front windshield. We screamed and braced ourselves. I clenched my eyes shut while keeping my hands on the wheel.

Sacrificial love meets needs in due season.

This dirt road had soaked up cloud spit for hours and was now ready to sweep my car straight across its two narrow lanes. My inexperienced driving left us high-centered on the lip of the ditch. The car teetered with the front wheels not touching the ditch and the back wheels gaining no traction on the road.

We were okay, only shaken up, thank God. After deliberating, we crawled into the back seat, Irene first. We opened the doors slowly, then three-two-one-jumped! Somehow, the car stayed balanced on the ditch's edge.

Laughing in relief, we slapped at the mud on our skirts.

Teetering Choices

We girls were in a pickle. We assessed: after dark, on a road with no traffic, with no money after burgers and sodas, in bad weather. No cell phones in 1970. Check.

What about interrupting a couple at the park to ask for a ride? Visions of the ensuing gossip at school drowned that idea.

"Okay, let's walk to the end of Osage. I'll call my dad there." I pointed toward the distant gas station. Daddy was a mechanic and had a winch on his work truck. *Reasonable, right? Except for the mile walk to the corner. But we were already soaked through. What other choice did we have?*

"No way! I'm not telling my parents!" Irene insisted. "They'd kill me! Let's call a wrecker. We'll get the money somehow. Or walk home! Please, God, could you send a taxi right now?" Irene begged. She finally landed in reality. "Okayyy, call your dad, but promise he'll never tell my dad. I'll be grounded for life!"

Although Irene had done nothing wrong, her mom lived in the state of "What if—?" My mom was more open-handed. I expected questions, maybe a lecture for the evening's shenanigans, possibly even grounding. Regardless, I couldn't imagine turning to anyone but my parents.

Agreeing to hike the distance, we grabbed our macrame hand-bags, linked elbows, and trekked. We were a sight when we trudged up to the gas station counter in all our dripping glory, giggling. We asked to use the phone. We didn't even have a dime for the pay phone!

A short conversation later, my dad was on his way. *He'll make it all better.*

Merciful Rescue

Dad and I dropped off my anxious friend at her home.

My dad saw every event as a season for a lesson. This night was no different. I would learn how to pull a car off high center, although I promised him over and over I'd never have to use this knowledge again. Grudgingly, I climbed from the back seat to the driver's seat, and Dad positioned his truck. The details are murky, but I remember Dad maneuvered over an hour in the mud to free my Chevy from its perch.

"Follow me." Dad passed my window, motioning toward his truck. He didn't take the usual route home, turning right instead of left at the end of Osage.

"Doesn't he know I want to be home?" I grumbled, wishing for hot cocoa and an afghan. Grouchy ingratitude had slithered in.

Dad turned into a convenience store lot (cocoa! yes!) but passed it and drove straight into a bay at the carwash. *What? He's going to wash his truck at this time of night!* He hopped out, pointed at me, and waved me into the next bay.

Ugh! He's got to be kidding! I pulled in, got out of my car, and slammed the door.

Dad handed me some quarters. "Here you go. Wash her up."

I stood there, gobsmacked, watching him stream soapy water onto his truck as I shivered in soaked sneakers. Earlier, the mental images that swamped me as I envisioned my consequences didn't include washing my car at midnight. Shouldn't "make it all better" include making me happy?

Dad instructed me how to crouch low to tease the caked mud off the wheel wells and wash the undercarriage. He did spare me from using the chamois, given the rain.

My baptism into responsibility that rainy night dripped revelation for years. My seventeen-year-old self didn't appreciate that clay washes off more easily when wet. But my dad knew, and sacrificial love meets needs in due season. A baby needs feeding when hungry, regardless of a mom's tiredness. A stranded teen needs rescuing, even in the rain. And people reach toward love when their abilities fall short.

P. S. I never utilized that lesson on moving a car off high center.

* All names in this chapter changed.

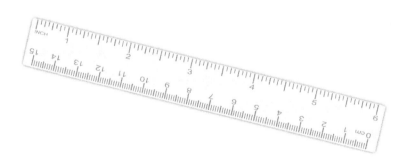

Down to a Dollar

by Lori Lipsky

*O*UR BALANCE AT the bank had fallen to one dollar. We were young, employed newlyweds, financially independent from our parents for the first time in our lives. The two of us disagreed whether a thousand dollars constituted an adequate savings buffer. One thousand dollars seemed like plenty of money to me. The more fiscally responsible half of our marriage disagreed.

Unable to find a teaching job despite my degree, I took part-time employment as a nanny for a young couple. My husband worked as a software programmer. We didn't carry a credit card. No one we knew did. They were a rarity in our circle at that time.

We paid monthly rent, utilities, a school loan payment, and a car payment. After writing checks for our bills each month, little remained. We slid into the easy habit of transferring money from savings into checking whenever our checking account balance neared zero.

An Unwelcome Challenge

My husband, Mark, happens to be a frugal soul. For the sake of marital harmony in those early years, I tried to be careful with spending. Still, I lacked the cautious tendencies of my spouse.

"We're down to a thousand in savings," he said to me one evening. "We should try to reduce our spending. I've read it's wise to reserve the equivalent of six months' wages to prepare for inevitable emergencies. Can we reserve savings for real emergencies and live off what's in checking? How about that goal?"

I froze, hoping the subject would magically change. It didn't. I was eager to avoid conflict in our marriage. My parents had sometimes argued about money when it came time to pay bills. I finally blurted out, "Six months seems impossible."

"Can we try?"

"We don't eat out. We never go bowling or to movies. We don't buy clothes. I'm not sure where it goes," I said.

"Let's try. Okay?"

I offered him a reluctant nod. The amount in our savings seemed more than adequate from my perspective. I wasn't as wound up about our finances as Mark was, but I would try. Maybe I could consolidate errands to save on gas.

Not long after the conversation, Mark phoned from work. "My car broke down. I found a ride to work. The mechanic says it's going to cost over six hundred to fix."

"Good thing we have a thousand in savings," I said.

God's kindness emboldened us to trust him all the more.

"You mean four hundred."

I groaned. "Four hundred."

Evaporating Savings

We transferred everything into checking and closed our savings account since the bank charged monthly fees for a low savings balance.

Three days later, Mark's Honda was fixed, but when I went out to start my old Buick, nothing. I turned the key several times. The mechanic towed the car to the service station to be fixed. Once we paid for

the automobile repairs, our checking account balance fell to one dollar. Thankfully, our check registry was accurate. Because I'd learned to keep careful balances after an overdraft experience, I knew with confidence that one dollar remained. No internet banking existed in those days, so keeping exact records was crucial.

Barren Cupboards

"Did you happen to ask your employers about an advance today?" Mark asked.

The warmth of a flush crept up my cheeks. "I couldn't do it. I know I told you I'd ask. Sorry."

He put his hand on my shoulder. "It's okay."

"Should we ask one of our parents?"

"Let's try to make it on our own."

I nodded in agreement.

"Have you checked the cupboards? Cereal makes a good staple," he said. His upbeat attitude helped mine. We were down to one dollar in the bank, but with God's help, we would make it until payday.

"The cereal's almost gone, and we don't have much milk. If only we had enough for those two things." Neither one of us had any cash left.

I continued. "We're not going to go hungry, but we might have some weird meals toward the end of the week. I counted two cans of soup, a box of mac and cheese, and a few of those little cans of baked beans. Plus, we have several slices of bread and some aging green grapes, but you're out of lunch meat. As you said, it'll be an adventure."

"I can take a can of beans to work for lunch," he said. "Monday's almost over. Payday is Friday. We should make it. What about your gas tank? Mine's over half. If we didn't work in opposite directions, we could carpool."

"I can't wait to celebrate payday by filling our tanks and getting groceries," I said. To celebrate payday each Friday, we usually shopped for food at the grocery store after cashing our checks at the bank. We enjoyed the time together. We never went on real dates, but being together was enough.

Unexpected Mail

The challenge was unlike any test we'd faced in our young marriage. We prayed, asking the Lord to help us make it through the week. We didn't ask the Lord for money. Where would it come from anyway?

A letter from our church arrived in our mailbox on Tuesday morning. Inside, I found a seven-dollar check. I called the office and learned it was payment for work I'd done as a nursery worker substitute for the Thursday women's Bible study. The receptionist apologized for the delay in sending the funds. The nursery work happened months earlier, but there had been a clerical error. I hadn't realized I'd be paid for the morning's work.

What incredible timing for seven dollars to appear! I purchased a dozen eggs, a gallon of milk, a loaf of bread, a package of bologna, and bananas. What an encouragement the unexpected check was to us. Waiting for Friday would be easy now. The surprise gift reminded us of the goodness of God. *Every good gift and every perfect gift is from above, coming down from the Father of lights* (James 1:17 ESV).

Our expensive back-to-back car troubles helped us learn to trust God to provide for our needs. They also helped confirm the importance of saving money for unexpected emergencies. After this experience, we made changes. Mark and I worked as a team to pay off our loans as fast as we could. Saving became a priority. After each payday, we gave a percentage to church, transferred a set amount into savings, paid our monthly bills, then lived on what remained.

Months later, we decided to avoid car loans as a next step. We opened a dedicated car savings account. This encouraged us to save even more—we never knew when a car might need to be replaced, and we could only spend as much as we'd saved for the next vehicle.

Receiving seven dollars in the mail was a wonderful encouragement. God lightened our load when we hadn't even asked him for money. He met our needs in a simple, generous way. This kindness emboldened us to trust him all the more.

Lessons from the Lanes

by Nancy Kay Grace

*P*RIDE SNEAKS INTO our lives at unexpected times and in unusual places, sometimes a bowling alley. I am not an avid bowler, but I enjoyed the sport while growing up in a family that participated in recreational leagues. And I have learned some lessons along the way.

The Fun of Pride

In college, my new boyfriend invited me to go bowling at the University Union. I had not bowled for several years, but I knew I was competent enough to have fun. I learned that Rick had bowled in leagues and was pretty good.

Oh—and I did have fun. Rick bowled his typical high score in our first game, and I had the highest score of my life—which was one pin more than his. I felt ecstatic! I'd never bowled so well with that many strikes and spares. Pride swelled within me—I'd beaten my boyfriend. And on our second date!

Of course, Rick did not share my joy. He looked directly at me,

stating, "Let's play two out of three." His bruised ego had to prove he was better—he did—and show that my high game was a fluke—it was. Rick's determination and skill kicked in with strike after strike.

He won the next two games as my arm weakened and my aim failed me. My scores for those two games were more typical of my slightly below-average ability. Sure, my pride was hurt, but I still owned the first game. And we still dated and later married.

> *When things don't go as expected, we can choose a response of agitation or acceptance.*

The Fall of Pride

Fast forward many years. Rick was now a pastor. We grew in our faith as we served in church ministry.

Once, we enjoyed some time away from the pressures of ministry at a retreat center in Colorado. The center had several recreational opportunities—hiking, swimming, and bowling. Bowling! Wouldn't it be fun to play a game or two, as we did in our early dating? And that's what we did.

We were the only people in the small bowling alley, so at least there wouldn't be an audience for any goof-ups. I hadn't donned the stylish bowling shoes for a while. As I tied them, I wondered if I'd end up sore after our fun afternoon.

It's simple and harmless, rolling a ball down the lane. That is until something unexpected happens in the usual movements of bowling. After my first step, my left foot stuck to the floor while at the same time, my right thumb remained secure in the ball as I tried to release it. The physics of momentum were in full swing, hurtling me forward in flight, parallel to the lane in Superwoman style. My hand let go of the ball, and it wobbled down the gutter. I landed in a not-so-graceful

heap, also in the gutter. At least I wore cute shoes.

As I was airborne, a little girl peered into the lanes and witnessed my flight and whole-body landing.

Wide-eyed, she asked, "Is that lady okay?"

I ignored her question, embarrassed that someone had observed me. I wondered how I tripped over the painted foul line and landed so far down the lane.

Laughing while struggling for composure, Rick answered, "Yeah, she'll be okay. She does this all the time."

The Follow-Up to Pride

My compassionate husband chuckled and helped me to my feet. (I can see the sermon title now—"Lifting Your Wife from the Gutter.") Thankfully, I sustained only a few minor scrapes and bruises from my episode of contact bowling.

Eventually, we composed ourselves. With our sides aching from laughter, we headed to the main office of the retreat center to let them know we were leaving the lanes. A cheerful staff person asked if we had signed the form releasing them from any injury liability. Had the little girl betrayed me, reporting my crash-landing bowling episode?

All we could do was snicker. We signed the forms. A few days later, we told the office staff why we thought it was so hilarious. The bruises on my knees and scraped elbows spoke for themselves.

Lessons from the Lanes

The Word of God teaches that we should be careful to avoid pride. *Pride goes before destruction, and haughtiness before a fall* (Proverbs 16:18 NLT).

With pride, we build ourselves up, often at someone else's expense. It's more accurate to have the self-awareness of being a work in progress rather than one who has it all together and is better than anyone else. My self-perception cannot be based on a one-time victory as a bowler. I'm glad my new boyfriend didn't allow my winning the

first game to derail our relationship. Instead, the incident spurred us to be comfortable with each other's personalities. We continue to laugh about it and other embarrassing episodes from life.

Events happen we cannot control. Life is often overwhelming. When things don't go as expected, we can choose a response of agitation from the problem or acceptance of the situation. Extremely high expectations limit or paralyze us. When my plans fell apart in planning a major celebration, my stress increased moment by moment. A friend kept my sanity in balance with the phrase, "It's all good." Those words—spoken to me frequently—helped me let go of my expectations. I gained a better perspective to accept the new plan. My tensions decreased, and I enjoyed the event.

Perfection is necessary in some areas of life, like surgery, but most of us don't handle scalpels every day. It's better for us to accept our imperfections while seeking excellence in whatever we do. We cannot take ourselves too seriously when we foul up or flop. I don't like mistakes, but they refine me. When I get embarrassed by some incident, I can fall into excessive self-judgment. A more appropriate response is extending self-grace to live with my goof-ups, even laughing at them.

Science has proven that laughter is beneficial to our health. The body releases endorphins when laughing. These are brain chemicals that help relieve stress, increase wellbeing, and raise oxygen levels. We all could loosen up and use a little more joy in our lives. Stress and tension start to fade when we find a way to laugh at ourselves. The well-known person, Anonymous, reminds us to keep the right perspective for handling pride. "Blessed are those who can laugh at themselves, for they shall never cease to be amused."

The lessons from the lanes? Set aside pride and perfectionism. Be willing to let go of things. Learn the skill of laughing at yourself. Enjoy the moment.

Oh, and be sure to wear knee pads when bowling.

One Stitch at a Time

by Carolyn Gaston

*H*AVE YOU EVER hopped into a new hobby or learned a new skill only to discover a powerful life lesson locked inside? That's what happened when my friend Cathy taught me how to make rag rugs during the pandemic.

By nature, I am a very social creature. I enjoy having people in my home. I love to spend time with friends from church. Getting together for food and fun makes me happy. It's deeply satisfying to bring people together. But, during the long pandemic, my social life came to a prompt and painful pause. I needed something to occupy the unrequested, unexpected alone time that invaded my home and life. I needed to keep my hands busy and to block my mind from focusing on fear. This drew me to become a rugger, aka a textile artist.

Try It

There are many methods of making rag rugs and a variety of names for them. The style of rug that Cathy taught me is known as the Amish

knot rug. Through the years, Amish women have used old shirts, threadbare bed sheets, worn-out dresses, and any extra fabric scraps they can find to make rugs for their homes. While my purpose is not to teach you to make a rag rug, I urge you to give it a try.

Trust that God creates extraordinary masterpieces.

You can find a plethora of YouTube videos that will teach you how to do this rewarding, relaxing craft. Simply search "Amish knot rug," "Swedish braided rug," "Scandinavian rug," or just "rag rug." This craft allows you to enjoy recycling and repurposing fabric as you carry on this old homestead tradition, producing colorful, one-of-a-kind area rugs. And maybe you can learn a life lesson too.

Learn It

Just how I craft a rag rug one special stitch at a time, God handcrafted me one marvelous detail at a time. In Psalm 139:13–15, we read the words of King David: *For you formed my inward parts; you knitted me together in my mother's womb. I praise you, for I am fearfully and wonderfully made. Wonderful are your works; my soul knows it well. My frame was not hidden from you when I was being made in secret, intricately woven in the depths of the earth* (ESV).

The Hebrew word for *fearful* implies honor and reverence, and the Hebrew word for *wonderful* means *set apart* or *unique*.[21] David praised God because he knew the miracle of God's handiwork very

---

21. Vivian Latigi, "Wonderfully Made" *In a New Light* (blog), December 29, 2021, https://inanewlight.co/2021/12/29/wonderfully-made/

well. He declared that God had made him reverently, shaping him intricately—unique and complex, absolutely beautiful and wonderful.

As I realize how unique and precious I am in God's sight, I can glorify him for his marvelous works as David did. David knew that God knew all about him even before he was born, and he believed God had created him with meticulous care. Just like David, I am amazing! God designed my brain unique, my body unique, my personality unique. He decided on my race, my fingerprints, and my special talents, even before I was born.

God creates each person with a distinct combination of abilities, interests, and style. In other words, he made you to be you. He made you so he could love you, and he made you to love him. As my friend Vickey shared with me, "Oh, the amazing complexity of the human body! God spoke and you were created."

Pray and Craft It

I let people know that while making rugs for them, I'm praying for them with each strip of fabric I cut, each snip of the scissors, each stitch, every loop, every print. After every completed journey around the rug, I ask God to bless them and help them see how incredibly beautiful they are—a unique, complex, perfect creation of God's hand.

Like a rug made from rags, perfect yet full of imperfections and irregularities. I thank God that he made them exactly who they are, and I ask him to show them that he has been with them every minute of their lives.

Even if I don't know who will receive the rug, God does; so, I pray for them too. When I gift it, I include a personal letter to encourage the recipient to embrace their uniqueness and to thank God for his unconditional love for them every time they look at the rug.

I remind them they were created on purpose for a purpose.[22] That God designed them just as my rugs are made—with individual detail and attention, not mass-produced, cookie-cutter items. I suggest they appreciate their uniqueness and never take for granted how intricately and meaningfully God made them. Each design in the rug results from a strip of fabric fitting in where it belongs, and each person can realize how they similarly fit into God's plan.

I want to motivate people to use their individuality for God's purpose. This unattributed quote says it all: "The two most important days in a man's life are the day on which he was born and the day on which he discovers why he was born." I believe God has a special message and mission custom-made for each of us.

If I were to give you a rug, this is the letter I would write to you.

22. Katherine Smith, "Fearfully and Wonderfully Made" *Katherine Smith* (blog), May 30, 2014, https://kaylsas.wordpress.com/2014/05/30/fearfully-and-wonderfully-made/

Dear friend,

I thank God that he made you to be you, exactly who you are. I've been asking him to show you that he has been with you in every loop of life. Please let this rug remind you that you are like a ceremonious symphony, a magical mélange of instrumental music. When you look at this rug, remember that you are like a chromatic kaleidoscope, a spectacular, symmetrical show of shapes and colors. When you place your feet on the rug, think about all the pieces that make it complete and think of yourself as a reward-winning recipe, replete with just the right ingredients.

You have been put together like no one else in the world. Thank God for the complex combination of your DNA—your temperament, voice, heartbeat, likes and dislikes, and hopes and dreams that make you a one-of-a-kind treasure.

Don't look at this rug and wish another color or a different fabric had been used. Just accept the rug as is and accept yourself as you are, valuable to God, unconditionally loved by him. Remember that God has orchestrated every chromosome in your body. There is only one you!

Day after day, stitch after stitch, God is faithful. Surrender yourself completely to God's loving hands, trusting that he creates extraordinary masterpieces!

Fearfully and wonderfully made,

Carolyn

Cinder Fire

by Becki James

I WOKE UP—TREMBLING. SWEAT saturated my pillow. Gulping air, I struggled to slow my breathing. Scanning the darkness, I saw lines formulate in the shadows, and I realized I lay safe in bed. *Another nightmare.* I panted. *It's all right. Those days are over.* Regaining a sense of reality, I wanted nothing more than to purge the presence of the past. But the vision knotted my gut with haunting realism. I shook my head, trying to break free. I knew there was no shutting my eyes now. The nightmare would pick up where it left off.

I heaved the covers, then shuffled to the bathroom. The motion sensor shot an amber glow across the tile. I mashed my fingers into my neckline, kneading away the images that left my skin clammy. Leaning over the sink, I dabbed water over my face, allowing the stream to cleanse the sandman's residue from my eyes. *Thank you, Lord, for running water,* I prayed, attempting to ground my thoughts.

Still, the mental pictures seemed as real as when they jarred me awake. I needed to break their power. Do something else. I stepped into the closet and rummaged through clothing, toppling some to the floor. I pulled leggings from the pile and threw a rumpled cardigan over my tee. *Might as well get up. It's probably almost morning anyway.*

My husband slept soundly in bed, unaffected by everything. He would sleep for at least another hour. I softly crossed the room to retrieve my phone from the charger. The screen lit, beaming the time with LED clarity.

God's living light fuels the ember within me so that I fan the flame of his purpose and joy.

Two a.m.? What? Not again. I sighed. *Will these nightmares ever stop?* Not that it mattered right now. I turned and slipped out the door.

The full moon rested low over the pond, casting light through the windows in the living area. I fumbled to start the Keurig. It gurgled, and I proceeded to the hearth to light a fire. With a warm ambience soon penetrating the room and a steaming mug in hand, I snuggled up on the couch and anticipated the sunrise.

Under Fire

Nightmares are like combustions of the past. They can relight painful memories. They have power to replicate vivid emotions, spiraling us backward. I am no longer physically trapped by the things that pop up in my dreams. God took me from a nightmare existence into a dreamy new life. Now peace is my companion.

Some have likened my story to a fairytale—one of heartache to happiness, ashes to advantage. They've nicknamed me Cinderella. While it is true that the fairytale girl received her happily-ever-after ending, that is not the high point for me. The good stuff of life is not what we end up with but who we become along the way. The underlying chronicle of Ella's character is the real meat of the tale. If I adopt any similarity to Cinderella, I want it to be her resilience under fire.

Cinders are remnants, partially burned but retaining combustible matter. They can either thrive or die, depending on where they lay in

the firebox. The more ash accumulates around them, the less oxygen flows to them. Forced to the dirtiest of chores, Cinderella was enslaved to the task of tending the fire. Her stepsisters took the oppression even further by blackening her name with a demeaning nickname. But Ella remained kind, despite their cruelty. They intended to mock her, but cinders are actually survivors! Her mindset was the oxygen that kept her healthy. And Ella retained her cinder fire.

Retaining Cinder Fire

In hindsight, I understand where parts of my past got buried in the ash of circumstance. When the people I loved turned on me, heaping up wounds, I had to find endurance. I had to learn to uncover spiritual health or be snuffed out by discouragement. My only option was to blow away the dust and allow the ember within to gain new strength.

The apostle Paul wrote to a young man named Timothy. People criticized Timothy, belittling him as Cinderella's stepfamily did to her. But Paul encouraged him, saying, *fan into flame the gift of God, which is in you through the laying on of my hands, for God gave us a spirit not of fear but of power and love and self-control* (2 Timothy 1:6–7 ESV). Like Timothy, I need to recognize the ember within myself as God's gift to me.

Fanning the Fire Within

When I see circumstances piling up around me, fear can smother me. Peace comes when I remember God stays with me. I am not alone. He gave me a spirit of power, not fear. When nightmares taunt me with past hurts or regrets, I remember where I stand. I am a survivor because God never left. God breathes composure over trials, fueling the girl on the inside of my story. My strength comes from him.

God created me and you as exclusive extensions of his image. We do not share identical souls. Nor do we share identical gifts. It has taken me half my adulthood to fan my gifts into flame. I spent years

121

standing in the residue of what burned me. Then I wasted time doubting myself. I was positioned in the ash.

The remnant within me—the one meant to ignite the next fire—needed to be uncovered. The cinder was there. But I lost sight of who God created me to be. When I saw his love for me, I began watching for him. I saw his light illuminating my little ember. Focusing on him was like opening the flow of fresh air. His love blew through my fears and helped me fan his living light within me.

Following the Living Light

Even storybook lives are riddled with heartache. Cinderella's happy ending mounted atop an ash heap of sadness—being orphaned, mistreated, and enslaved in her own home. Even her little bird friends could not chirp away every bad memory. Maybe, if she were a real person, Cinderella would have occasional nightmares like mine. But since she's only a make-believe character, I choose to look beyond the feel-good conclusion of the tale and note the fierce maiden with the fire of kindness within her. That light illuminated the tragedy around her. In my book, that holds far more worth than castles, carriages, or priceless glass slippers.

Yes, I will take that reference, likening my life to the fairytale—call me Cinder-Becki if you wish. I want what glows within me to radiate from the living light of God. He is the significance of my story. The rest is merely glitter that pales in comparison to knowing he loves me. Love like this ignites my joy. I will gladly fan that flame.

Soot and grime may come my way, but I will retain the resilience to kindle new flames. God's living light fuels the ember within me so that I fan the flame of his purpose and joy.

The next time I am jolted by the nightmares of life, I will stoke the fire—my cinder fire—and feel God's presence warm me with his love.

The Little Guys

by Carin LeRoy

I OPENED A FORTY-FOUR-POUND metal drum of flour and began to gather the remaining items to bake bread. As I went to scoop out the flour needed, something seemed strange, so I took a closer look.

Is the flour moving?

I gasped. Little grubs squiggled in the flour. I took a step back when the stale odor from the drum hit my nostrils. This was beyond anything I wanted to use for baking. But since I wasn't in charge of the household, I went to check with the lady of the house, Mrs. Merri.

As new missionaries in our twenties, my husband and I lived for nine months with an older couple for a time of orientation to our new country. The little river town, Kiunga, had occasional generator power, a few stores, and even a small hospital. Mission leadership had placed us under the couple's guidance. It became my responsibility to keep the table supplied with freshly baked bread. Store-bought bread was expensive and not readily available, so I enjoyed the new challenge.

Accepting My New Assignment

I walked to her office, where she sat working.

"Mrs. Merri," I said, "I just opened the drum of flour. It's stale and has worms. Do we have better flour to make bread?"

She stopped her work and walked into the kitchen with me. Her brow furrowed as she peeked into the drum. I lifted a spoonful to show her the wiggles in the flour.

"Well," she said, "it's all the flour we have. You'll have to sift out the worms."

Really? Sift out worms?

I signed up for missionary service, but I didn't know this would be in the job description. Not only was I dealing with unrelenting heat, strange foods, a new language, and unfamiliar customs, I had to sift worms out of flour before making bread.

It was a necessity to be endured.

> *Contentment accepts tough times, rejoices in blessings, and realizes both are given to us by God.*

Although the drum of flour had never been opened, it was old flour that had been in storage for a while. The supplies we found in town were often past their expiration date. We ate chewy cheese puffs, white-spotted chocolate, and other items past their prime. Sometimes older supplies were sent upriver to remote areas once newer supplies had arrived in port cities.

Sifting Out Worms

Determined to be a brave new missionary, I reached for the wire strainer. Then I pitched in a cup of flour, grabbed a spoon, and started sifting—slowly. Flour fell into the bowl below. As the sifter emptied, I started to see wiggly little white grubs coated with flour. I dumped them onto a plate on the counter, where they squirmed in a heap. Then

I gathered another scoopful and started the process again.

It took forever to sift the eight cups needed because I didn't want one single worm to escape. If one made it past the sifter, I snatched it out with a spoon and chucked it onto the pile with the rest of the little guys. I shuddered to think about one worm in my bread and refused to think about the other "additions" that came from worms living in flour.

After a few months of bread-making, extracting worms from flour became tedious work. Sifting quicker seemed a better option. I knew a few were making it past the sieve when my chuck-out pile was smaller than my earlier efforts. Though the kneading process was sure to send them on to worm heaven.

Making the Best of a Difficult Situation

Although she didn't like it, I knew Mrs. Merri had learned over her long missionary career to tolerate many circumstances. She knew that whining and complaining were futile in a situation you couldn't change. I still needed to learn that, but her example and patience helped show me how to make the best of this situation.

I learned missionaries could adapt to things over time because I noticed that some long-serving ones didn't worry about sifting flour. We were invited to another missionary station twenty-five miles away for lunch with another couple one weekend. After we sat around the table, the host prayed, and we began to eat. Lunch consisted of boiled eggs sliced into a white sauce and served on toast. I took several bites before noticing a few cooked worms in the sauce.

Obviously, worm sifting wasn't high on her priority list. She had adapted. Picking them out from a cream sauce wasn't a good option either, although I tried to shove them around my plate. I ate carefully, trying not to be obvious, and managed to get through the meal. My husband, however, never noticed a thing and ate lunch with gusto. That reminded me of the old saying, *ignorance is bliss.*

Being Thankful for Little Things

The drought broke and the rains started months later. With the river high enough for the boats to travel, they brought new supplies to our little jungle town. It was a great day when fresh, worm-free flour arrived. I never took good flour for granted again, and I had learned what it meant to become thankful for these little things in life.

What is my response when I find myself in an unpleasant circumstance? Am I willing to adjust, or do I whine and complain? If I cannot change the circumstance, the best choice is to learn to adapt and submit to where God has placed me. We don't have to like it, but we can learn to accept it. I am reminded of the words of King Solomon when he said, *Enjoy prosperity while you can, but when hard times strike, realize that both come from God. Remember that nothing is certain in this life* (Ecclesiastes 7:14 NLT).

Challenging times not only give me the opportunity to accept a difficult circumstance, but they also give me more awareness of blessings that come my way. A heart trained to find contentment learns to receive tough times, to rejoice in the blessings of good times, and to realize that God gives us both in his loving sovereignty.

I never liked sifting worms, but I did gain a new appreciation for the benefits of fresh flour. Hard things have a way of giving us a new perspective.

Feel-Good, Bad Things

by Mindy Cantrell

*E*VER HAD ONE of those times when you did something you knew you shouldn't do, but temptation got the best of you, and you did it anyway? And oh my, for a little while, it felt really good. Yes, one of those times. Maybe it went something like this?

Temptation comes along. You throw caution to the wind and dive right in. Now, a smile cracks your face, and the big bad world ceases to exist for a moment. *Mmmm, I like this!* Good feelings flow through your body, and you savor the satisfaction. Then, wait! What's that feeling trying to sneak up in there? Is that guilt? *Oh, no, you don't!*

You quickly swat that guilty feeling away like a bug before it gets any closer. *Whew!* Then, you continue doing that feel-good, bad thing. *Oooh yeah.* It feels so good as you silence that guilty voice and carry on.

Guilt Jumps Up and Bites

Ow! Get away from me! That bite took a little of the feel-good out of that bad thing, didn't it? So, what do you do? You quickly stomp out that guilt and let that feel-good flow again. *Aah!*

> *God's forgiveness and grace wash over me. The walls fall. I am free and clean once more.*

You're settling in, enjoying yourself once more, and then—guilt bites again! This time, it really gets you. And not merely guilt but also suspicion rises up in your heart. There might be a valid reason you shouldn't be doing this feel-good thing. *Maybe this is truly bad for me.* Since you like it, though, you throw up excuses. *Everyone's doing it, so why can't I? It makes me feel good.* As you wobble on this tightrope of good and bad, you envision your future self after the feel-good, bad effects have taken root. *Whoa! I don't want to be like that!*

So, you grudgingly stop and walk away, rubbing your heart where guilt left its mark. You find yourself relieved that you mustered the strength to step away from that feel-good, *bad* thing.

However, later, that mark from guilt throbs again. It accuses you: *You dummy! You fell for that temptation again!* On the defensive now, you yell, *So what? It's not like it affects anyone but me.* Then, wham! It slams you hard. Regret and guilt pile up. They tear you down.

What's wrong with me? Why can't I just say no? You doubt yourself. *Maybe I'm not a good person, because I like it.* You begin to feel hopeless. Unworthy. Bad!

This is where I was yesterday. I gave in to that familiar temptation—*again*. I eagerly jumped in headfirst, overflowing myself with this feel-good, *bad* thing. What was I thinking? Who knows. All I knew was I loved this feel-good, bad thing. And I wanted it. It soothed me. We all *need* feel-good things that soothe us sometimes, right?

The Tug-of-War Ensues

I mean, this thing felt really *good* while it lasted. It put a smile on my face. Though, I'll admit, only for a short time. Then guilt set in, deep

down, in all those conflicting stages. Feel good. Guilt. Excuses. Guilt. Relief. *Idiot!* Unworthiness. Shame. Sound familiar?

So, today, my guilt mark had me consumed with these conflicting thoughts. I realized in my heart that no matter how much I enjoyed it, this feel-good thing would not have a good effect on me. I asked myself, *Is this little bit of feel-good worth the guilt, negative feelings, and unbecoming behavior this bad thing will ultimately have on me?* Hmmm.

How I hate this emotional tug-of-war. I sure don't need any help feeling down about myself because I already have too many imperfections to deal with. 'Cause, you know, God didn't make me perfect. Wink, wink.

And speaking of God. Is God mad at me? Should I hide from him until I can get past this? *I feel so unworthy. I'm so confused!* My conscience reminded me I shouldn't do that feel-good, *bad* thing, but I did it anyway. I rebelled. I turned my head the other way and gleefully jumped right in. I messed up. So, now what?

It's Time for a Feel-Good Conversation

I wrestled with it and concluded I should talk to God. I needed to tell him what I had done, that I wanted to feel close to him again, but my guilt had built a wall between us. I realized he already knew, but I needed to verbalize it so it wouldn't become a self-destructive secret.

"Dear God," I prayed. "I don't know why I keep falling into this same thing, over and over. Please forgive me. Please take away these awful guilty and unworthy feelings so I can experience your closeness again. I know, God, that you never leave me—rather, it is I who turns away from you. But I'm back now. Will you take my hand and lead me again? This time I'm gonna hold on tight."

God's forgiveness and grace wash over me. The walls fall. I am free and clean once more.

And once again, I'm in that feel-good, *good* place! Oh, thank you, God, that you are so willing and able to provide this *good* thing

for me every time I ask. Without it, I'm a mess! This verse sums up my prayer perfectly. *Create in me a clean heart, O God, And renew a right and steadfast spirit within me* (Psalm 51:10 AMP).

You see, I needed my heart cleansed of the guilt and my spirit renewed with forgiveness. I needed to gain perseverance to not fall into that temptation again.

The Feel-Good *Good* Wins

Through these experiences, I learned that we have feel-good, *good* things, and feel-good, *bad* things. It's up to us to choose which ones we'll participate in. I don't think we have the willpower to always choose the *good* thing because so often, the *bad* thing makes us feel so *good*.

Whether it's overindulging in rich chocolate or yummy comfort food and drink, choosing sizzling novels and media, or pursuing inappropriate relationships and activities—we fall into these tempting, feel-good, *bad* things. We excuse them away as self-care, stress relief, or ways to let off steam. Though they may soothe our tired and wounded souls for a moment, as I found out, they usually cause more heartache. For me, it was that little devil guilt that kept jumping up and biting me until I was an insecure, hopeless mess, even doubting that I could be a good person. It's pretty hard to let your light shine when you feel like that.

Thank goodness for the voice of holy conviction, which, unlike guilt and its condemning words, told me to simply confess my waywardness and get it off my chest. Instead of swimming in shame, I found myself bathing in the refreshment of a cleansed heart and mind. As a bonus, I found I wasn't tempted by that feel-good, *bad* thing anymore. Now *that's* a feel-good, *good* lesson!

The Last Valentine's Gift

by Charlaine Martin

*T*EARS WELLED UP while browsing Facebook and sipping my coffee this morning. In Memories, a post from five years ago pricked my heart. This memory from shortly after my first husband's death felt surreal. My breath stopped for a moment. It was the Valentine's Day gift I inadvertently gave him a few months after he died. I had avoided the thought of my first Valentine's Day without him, so I ignored it altogether. Frozen, I stared at the screen as tears spilled onto my cheeks. Then, my thoughts drifted back to our first Valentine's Day as newlyweds.

Don and I had gifted each other cute Valentine's cards and gifts ever since I was sixteen. We married in college, our hearts fluttering with newlywed bliss. Early into our first year as Mr. and Mrs., Valentine's cards and gifts flooded the store where I worked as a cashier. I adored the bright reds, pinks, and purples. Love was certainly in the air. That Valentine's Day together was special because we had recently sealed our love with our vows and rings in our hometown church. It

seemed like yesterday. This is how I remember events unfolding after Don and I compared stories later.

Newlyweds Celebrate Love

Don, such a romantic, had hurried to find the perfect expression of his love. The grocery store's floral department greeted him with brilliant-colored roses. Some were elaborate bouquets, while others stood gracefully solo in glass vases trimmed with satin bows. The vast array of choices overwhelmed him. Limited by our meager funds, he scanned the display for something in our budget.

After deliberation, he finally chose a fresh pink rose. "I'd like that one," he pointed it out to the florist with a smile. She wrapped it in floral paper and handed it to him.

While he walked to his car with a twinkle in his eye, he thought, *Won't Char be surprised to find this after work!* This prized rose lay in the passenger seat of his rusty green hatchback as he drove down the wintery-slushed street.

No matter what we do, sorrow waits until it catches us in the quietness of our souls.

Later that evening, Don pulled my spare key out of his coat pocket, trying not to drop it in the snow of the store's parking lot while I helped last-minute shoppers inside. Grinning, he opened my car door to place it on my steering wheel, but it wouldn't cooperate. Perplexed, he tried to weave its stem through the steering wheel but gave up.

Finally, sighing in resignation, Don perched it precariously on top so I would find it when I got in my car. Then he dashed home to wait for me.

Disappointments Can't Extinguish Love

Snowflakes danced under the parking lot lights in the frigid night air. I could see my breath ahead of me as I scurried to my car after the store

closed, toting a bag with a heart-shaped box of his favorite chocolates and a Valentine's Day card I bought at lunch. I slipped into my car and carefully drove home on the slick streets. My heart overflowed with excitement.

Once I arrived home, I trotted up the stairs to our apartment, set my bag on a chair, and removed my snow-glittered coat. Don relaxed on the sofa facing our door while waiting for me. Beaming, he asked, "Well?"

"Hi, Hon! Umm, what?" I raised an eyebrow pondering, *Did I forget to pick something up at the store?*

"Did you find your Valentine's Day gift?" Don inquired, a hint of concern in his voice.

"No. Why?" I hesitated.

"Oh, no! It was on your steering wheel," he groaned. He sprang to his feet, pulled on his coat, and ran out our apartment door. After a moment, he returned with a smooshed pink rose. What a pitiful sight as it dripped dirty, melted snow. My boots had soiled its pretty paper. Obviously disappointed, he gave it to me with a hug and kiss. "I was afraid it might fall off your steering wheel. I just wanted to surprise you. Happy Valentine's Day! I love you!"

"Thank you. I love you too! It looks beautiful." Carefully, I tried to revive this bedraggled gift of love. We exchanged cards with hugs and kisses, and then I gave him his chocolates. What a lovely evening together at home.

Death Can't Kill Love

I continued reminiscing over the years of our marriage, sitting with my computer still spotlighting that Facebook memory. We enjoyed giving each other fun love offerings such as pun-filled cards and hokey gifts. We read them together, snickering as we snuggled. One year he gave me a funny-looking stuffed creature. When I pressed the heart on its

hand, it played a cheesy rendition of "Love Will Keep Us Together." Although our gifts were silly, what mattered was the love we shared.

Then my mind wandered deeper into that Facebook memory. After Don's death, I had intentionally ignored the stores' pink, red, and purple heart decorations. That evening, I came home from work at the health club with achy legs. An eerie emptiness filled the apartment while I took off my coat and boots. My fluffy orange cat wound around my feet, purring as if to say, "Welcome home!" I smiled and petted his soft head.

I sank into my comfy sofa to check email with my laptop. One grabbed my attention. At first, I hesitated with my finger poised over the mouse button. Then, sighing, I clicked it open. It was the monument company I had contacted a few days earlier. They requested that I finalize the last detail for Don's burial place. I found a contract attached with a headstone design, awaiting my approval. Since they needed my prompt response, I replied, "It looks fine. Go ahead." Mechanically, I printed the contract, signed it, and put it in an envelope to mail back.

Suddenly stunned, I realized it was Valentine's Day. Tears flowed down my cheeks as grief washed over me. No more fun cards or cute gifts, nor snuggles and giggles together. Instead, memories haunted me, like the last time we cuddled in his hospital bed after nurses had removed all the tubes and wires from his cancer-wracked body. And then his move to hospice. I felt as if an invisible hand had ripped my heart out of my chest.

I curled up with my cat, sobbing. "Mrrrow?" my faithful feline nuzzled under my arm. No matter how hard I tried, I couldn't avoid grief.

It seemed crazy that I gave Don a stately gray headstone with his photo on it for Valentine's Day. My Facebook post stated, "What a very odd Valentine's Day. I just signed the contract for Don's headstone." This was my final gift of love.

Time Turns Grief into Beautiful Memories

Reflecting back, I could see how dodging grief only delayed it. No matter what I did, sorrow waited until it caught me in the quietness of my soul. I learned how mourning morphs over time from a gut-wrenching emptiness to wistful, beautiful memories of a life well-loved. I am so blessed because we shared tremendous love all those years.

As I leaned back in my chair, sipping my coffee, a misty-eyed smile slowly spread across my face. *Thank you, Lord, for these precious memories with Don.*

Losing Bobby

by Mary Curcio

*P*ARENTING CHILDREN IS truly a blessing—yet it can be a challenge for single parents. Thankfully, my children grew up with two parents, but my mom didn't have that blessing. I worried about her. As a single parent, Mom raised four children and managed a household, all while working a full-time job. Busy raising my five daughters, I wasn't able to offer much support.

Building a Bond of Love

My youngest brother struggled without his father. A handsome boy becoming a man at seventeen, he looked like a young Erik Estrada. He was a bit mischievous and loved to putter with treasures found on his searches.

His antics were mostly harmless. Until that day Bobby puttered with a cigarette lighter and a can of gasoline. Within seconds he was on fire.

I received a frantic call from my sister. Bobby was in a severe burn unit with seventy percent of his body covered in third-degree burns.

Every day our hearts thought we would hear the words that Bobby didn't make it. We wondered how we would live without him. His screams of pain as they debrided him still haunt my memory today.

His recovery was slow and steady, as was this new relationship we were developing. Every weekend, I drove one hundred miles to visit him in the hospital. I delivered games to play, his favorite food to eat, and new music to enjoy. He was beginning to be happy again. The time we spent with him is an investment I'll never regret. I can still see the smile on his face. Every time I visited, his first question was, "What did you bring me to eat?" He was really saying, "I love you, Sis."

Becoming a Responsible Brother

Eventually, Bobby healed enough to come home. Even though seventy percent of his body was burned, his face bore no scars. I often wondered why Bobby wasn't bitter or mad for what happened to him. In fact, his sense of humor was funnier and sharper than ever. His wit and charm still made us laugh. My girls loved him. He made them laugh so much that they asked me if I would allow him to become their babysitter.

Taking care of four girls and one nursing two-month-old is a big responsibility for anyone to take on. Our relationship was growing, and I could see he was doing well. We loved having him in our home, so I decided to give him a chance as a babysitter. He was ready for a challenge, and I was ready for a night out.

God's boundaries don't fence us in, but rather they say, "I love you."

So out I went. I left Bobby with all the instructions—written down of course. I listed every phone number he could possibly need and the addresses where I would be. I gave the girls their "better be

good or else" instructions. If they wanted Bobby to be their babysitter, they had better behave.

When I arrived home, the house was clean and in order. The girls were in bed, and the nursing baby was a little fussy. Bobby shared how the evening went. He let me know the girls had been a breeze, but he was disappointed the baby had been fussy. "Mary, she doesn't like me. She wouldn't take the bottle from me."

I reassured him he did a great job. "Don't worry, Bobby, she doesn't like anyone who can't nurse her."

Setting Boundaries for a Brother

That school year wasn't going well for Bobby, and it wasn't going well at home. He partied and refused to follow my mom's rules. I was worried about him, so I invited him to live with us for the summer. He was thrilled, but I was clear that he would have chores, household rules to follow, and a curfew. We didn't have an extra bedroom, but he never complained about sleeping on the floor.

Bobby did question why I set a curfew. He pressed the issue many times, but I was clear that he had to be in every night by ten o'clock. He felt my curfew was unreasonable because it was summer. I consistently reminded him that he could choose to go back home or obey our curfew. One night, still complaining about the curfew and annoying the family while we were all trying to watch TV, I beckoned him into the kitchen. I hoped reasoning with him would help. "Bobby, you have to come home by ten because I can't go to bed if I know you aren't home. I can't sleep until I know you are safe.

I thought the matter was settled, but one summer night, the loud rumbling of cars without mufflers could be heard through the whole neighborhood. Looking out the window, I saw a bunch of young teenage boys with their hot rods in my driveway. They asked if Bobby could come outside. I heard low murmuring as if they were conjuring up something. A mother can tell.

I felt myself getting anxious. Assuming Bobby would leave with

his friends, I hoped I had enough stamina to tell him he couldn't go with them if it went past his curfew. My girls anxiously watched. They knew Bobby had a curfew, and they didn't want him to leave.

Bobby came inside to ask for permission to leave with his friends. Knowing how important this was to him, I struggled to hold firm to my conviction. After all, he had been very good this summer—completing his chores and helping with the girls. Looking at him while my family looked at me, I let him know he couldn't come back here. It was too close to ten o'clock, so I knew he couldn't make his curfew.

The screen door slammed as Bobby went back outside. Concerned for his safety, I got up to call my mom to let her know he wouldn't be with us that night. As I reached for the phone, I heard the screen door close again.

Bobby had chosen not to go out with the guys.

Relieved, we all got up and hugged him. His smile said he knew that I loved him and wanted what was best for him. Most of all, I was proud of him for learning to appreciate my boundary of love. He'd discovered that boundaries don't fence us in, but rather, they say, "I love you."

Saying Goodbye to Bobby

Summer ended, and Bobby's senior year was about to begin. We shopped for clothes and school supplies before moving him back home, where he had his own bed and desk. We hoped he would have a successful school year. School started on a Wednesday, but two days later, Bobby was killed when leaving a party late at night on the back of a motorcycle.

That summer taught me the necessity of setting boundaries for Bobby and for my children. Though my heart was broken at losing Bobby, my convictions about boundaries for my children didn't waver. More important, God showed me that his boundaries are boundaries of love for us.

Intense Loss, Immense Comfort

by Hally Wells

*M*OM AND I chatted about the previous weekend's activities. My mother, always a gifted listener and tireless encourager, was working in her office at the county courthouse, and I was enjoying life as a stay-at-home mother of a kindergartener and a toddler. I heard one of her staff enter and tell her she had a call. Mom asked that she take a message—she'd return the call in just a bit.

Within moments, that same employee returned. "Melba, it's Dennis Tucker."* Those are the words I most remember hearing.

Mom said she'd call me back shortly.

But, over the next fifteen minutes or so, my mind wrestled with the words I'd heard. My parents had been divorced for twenty years by this time. And, though they were always friendly, respectful, and never said an unkind word about the other, it was odd that my paternal uncle was calling my mother—his former sister-in-law. It was around 10:00 a.m. on March 10, 2003.

My father had passed away suddenly that morning. A fatal heart attack struck him in the early hours of that Monday. He was sixty-one

years old, and I was thirty-eight. The call to my mother had come quickly. My father's co-workers had been convinced something was amiss when he hadn't called or arrived to work by 8:15. Dad called in sick only three days in thirteen years. They knew something wasn't right.

They'd contacted my father's girlfriend, she'd contacted my father's brother, and the news had traveled fast. By the time my mother arrived at my door not long after hanging up with me, I practically knew what the message would be. I just knew.

Sudden Loss

Nothing wrecked me like losing my dad. My parents' divorce during my first year of college had left me forever changed. It was a stigmatizing event in 1983, and I had come to view my family differently. We were now part of a club that was "less than" the family I once thought we were.

While the anguish of losing my dad was immense, so was the comfort from my heavenly Father.

I felt the ache of loneliness, and my trust in God faltered during an extended season of singleness throughout my twenties. Impatient, I wondered if I would ever find the right man and have a family of my own. Later, infertility treatments, a miscarriage, and an adoption journey taxed me physically and emotionally. I couldn't help but wonder why everything was so ridiculously hard.

Dad's passing, though, had sent me crashing into my own mortality. I grieved the relationships my father would never have with his grandkids. I mourned that he would never have a retirement—a large celebration after thirty-plus years with his company and the years of rest and reward following. I missed my dad tremendously. However, I never doubted where he was, where he landed after taking his final breath.

I imagined Dad picking the brains of Mickey Mantle and Elvis Presley, riding horses, and joking and telling stories with old friends. I knew, too, that if heaven had chores—a fence or project to build, a yard to mow, a dirty task to be done—Dad would be doing it in the same methodical and meticulous way he did everything.

Wonderfully Big, Little Things

While the anguish of losing my dad was immense, so was the comfort provided by my heavenly Father. He alone knew the loss that my family and I felt, and he blessed me with peaceful treasures each step of the way.

The first of those came on the day of Dad's visitation when my husband, a practical and skeptical first-generation German-American, observed something as he wrestled my daughter's white tights onto her. He watched her, a child who rarely spoke, turn her head toward the window of her room, smile, and say "Paw Paw" just as if he'd appeared to her at that very moment. Though I had not witnessed the event, Tim's observation and sharing of it were meaningful.

In the weeks leading up to my father's death, he'd made two seemingly inconsequential comments. I recalled them in my grief and became certain that God had caused my father to say those words that would eventually be so comforting. In one instance, he had said emphatically, "I have lived life." That was huge to me.

In another conversation between my father, sister, and I, Dad spoke about how he'd tried to mend old wounds and do for those he'd neglected during a particularly difficult time. I assured him he'd righted any wrongs, made up for any slights that might have existed. He agreed, saying, "I think I'm about there." These words acted as a salve to my broken heart.

Ways He Leads

My sister and I arranged our father's funeral with help from family and my father's girlfriend, whom he had dated for ten years before his

death. They'd spent the evening before he died with another female friend who had lost her husband some months earlier. We learned later that they had talked about angels and heaven. While Dad didn't have perfect health, I don't believe he expected to go home the next day.

My sister and I had given Dad a sixtieth birthday party a year prior. We hosted a small but extra special family event. One meaningful element was creating a video of photos from Dad's life. I presented a speech ala *This Is Your Life*, my sister demonstrated her acting skills in a skit, and we made a scrumptious meal. It was all a surprise. Dad later said that he "could have been taken to Italy and wouldn't have enjoyed it any more!" I wholeheartedly believe that God led us to have that birthday celebration. The video played all evening at Dad's visitation, and we were grateful that we'd hosted that special party for him.

Perfect Timing

Dad's girlfriend suggested having a particular local woman sing at the funeral. My father had heard her sing at other services, actually making a point to compliment her and ask her if she'd sing at his funeral one day. It may have been a playful comment, but it was remembered and shared at just the right time.

Especially ironic was that after my dad's funeral service, that soloist recalled where she'd seen my father years earlier. Betsy* had been in a single-car accident. Though not seriously hurt, she was also not fully aware. A man had come upon the scene and waited with her until help arrived. My father was the man who had stayed with her—the one who had quietly left when emergency workers came.

I may not have recognized my heavenly Father's presence when my parents divorced, when I was single and lonely, or when I endured infertility, but I felt it in abundance when my earthly father died. And I learned that we are never alone—most assuredly not in our darkest times!

* Name changed.

Lessons from Faded Scars

By Denise Margaret Ackerman

WHAT DO A dog bite, barbed wire, and melted mortar have in common? My encounters with each of them left me with a significant scar and, more importantly, a valuable lesson learned.

Dog Bite

Warm rays of sunlight filtered through the green canopy of maple trees lining the tranquil street in front of my grandparents' village home. As country girls, my older sister Debbie and I felt as if we were in a metropolis as we skipped along the uneven sidewalk. We were careful not to step on any cracks (so as not to break our mother's back).

We were delighted when our exploring led us to a furry four-legged creature. Debbie was the first to stroke his soft, curly brown fur. Not wanting to miss out, I boldly stepped toward our new acquaintance, but before I reached him, my sister alerted me to the dog's growing displeasure. "You'd better not pet him."

I ignored her stern warning and his angry snarl, defiantly proclaiming, "If you can pet him, so can I." My next memory was waking

up on Grandma's sofa with a pounding headache and five painfully tight stitches above my right eye. Why did I refuse to listen to someone older and wiser?

Rebellious at heart, I often find myself resistant to the unsolicited advice of others. I need the Lord's help to humble my stubborn heart and be willing to accept the counsel of others. Standing before the mirror each morning preparing for the day, I pray that the prominent scar on my forehead will remind me to respect wise guidance.

Barbed Wire

It was an unforgettable Fourth of July. Mom's out-of-state relatives were visiting our farm. For hours we played hide-and-seek with cousins we rarely ever saw. When the evening sky darkened, we began chasing fireflies. Laughter filled the air as we held mason jars aloft, trying to capture the iridescent lightning bugs. Wooden posts, strung with barbed wire, surrounded the pasture where we played. I discovered a long strand of coiled barbed wire obscured by the tall grass and shouted a warning to the others. But then, caught up in the challenge of capturing our bounty, the barbed wire snared a victim—me.

Cousin Mike, my hero, swooped me up in his arms and carried me through the meadow and down the back lawn to our farmhouse kitchen. Dad pinched together the deep wounds on my leg using multiple bandages to stop the bleeding. Sitting there enduring the pain, I rehearsed the series of events in my mind. Even though I was the one who discovered the snare and warned everyone about it, I was the one who got hurt. How could the danger I had uncovered only moments earlier be so quickly forgotten?

> I need the Lord's help to humble my stubborn heart.

It is so easy to get swept away by the exciting distractions the world offers. Just like barbed wire, these enticements can become a snare that entraps. Something as simple as a shiny new credit card can entice me to overspend. Getting caught up in the joys of shopping, I can quickly forget the dangers of buying more than I can afford. A painful consequence arrives when those bills come due.

The jagged scars on my leg remind me to stay alert to the Enemy's distractions that can entrap me with devastating results.

Melted Mortar

My childhood dream was to become a secretary like my beautiful and successful Aunt Mary. My first clerical position was in the field office trailer at a nuclear power plant under construction in our area. My secretarial duties varied from typing quality control inspection reports to processing new employee paperwork.

It was not the glamorous job of my dreams. Daily, the alarm sounded, alerting staff to vacate the office trailer as the construction company dynamited away layers of rock in the area that would later house the reactor. Already hardened to a callous work environment, I didn't hesitate to request a transfer to the concrete testing lab to work as a technician for a higher rate of pay.

The functions of the technician position were physically demanding and required lifting, categorizing, and performing compression tests on large concrete cylinders. Once the cement had cured, we ladled melted sulfur mortar into a mold. Then we carefully placed the heavy cement tube into the hot substance. Once cooled, technicians struck the side of the cylinder with a rubber mallet, releasing it from the form. We repeated the process for the opposite end.

We performed the compression test by inserting the capped, smooth-ended concrete cylinder into a large machine that crushed it, measuring the pounds per square inch the cement could withstand.

I began to question this career move in the shocking moment

when one of those heavy cylinders slipped through my hands and splashed hot mortar painfully across my forearm. As one of the technicians drove me to the emergency room to get the adhered mortar removed, I asked myself a motive-revealing question, "Is this lab work worth the two dollars per hour pay raise?"

The possible hazards or negative aspects involved in the technician's job had never occurred to me before making the impulsive decision to push away from my desk. The grueling lab facility was a far cry from the nonstrenuous clerical work the office required. I pursued this new line of work solely because the wage was greater.

As a spontaneous person, I sometimes make hasty decisions. Even though this characteristic is woven into my temperament, it's possible to make wise choices by memorizing God's Word, seeking his wisdom, and consulting a godly mentor before making a life-altering move. The Word of God instructs me to *get all the advice and instruction you can, so you will be wise the rest of your life* (Proverbs 19:20 NLT). The large, somewhat faded scar on my arm reminds me to stop, pray for wisdom, and seek godly counsel before I act.

Valuable Lessons

Reflecting on the cause of my injuries sustained in the three encounters reveals much about my fallen nature. I succumbed to fleshly desires that I cannot fight or change in my own strength. God sent his Son, Jesus, to pay the price for sin. When I repented and turned away from my sin, I received the forgiveness that Jesus offers to all who place their lives in his hands. I opened my heart to the indwelling of the Holy Spirit. By his Spirit, I receive strength, guidance, and the power to walk with God rather than according to my flesh.[23]

What scars do you bear that can serve as a powerful lesson from God's classroom?

---

23. Romans 8:1

Stage Fright

by Nancy Graves

*T*HEY STARED AT me. Cold, lifeless eyes. Like tiny mirrors re-flecting my empty soul. I could see the flame of life dwindling. It was a party like hundreds before, and all my friends were there. Dr. Miller, Teddy, Miss Kitty and her brood, Charlie, and others. We went way back—as far as I could remember. I brought them and seated them—and propped them upright. They were my stuffed animals. But to that point in my young life, they were family!

I remember the day well.

I sat surrounded on the thin parquet floor of my bedroom, less than an inch off the slab of our garden apartment. It always seemed cozy there before, filled with sparkling conversation, friendship, and great adventure. But this day, assembled before the makeshift table of proper tea ware, silence chilled the air. Like waking from a lovely dream of happy times and laughter, I sat awakened, eyes wide to the fact that I was alone. I always had been.

But I don't want to grow up! My remnant inner child refused to let go and wrestled with time, the culprit. Valiantly, she tried to revive the beloved friends who had journeyed beside her through thick and thin,

embodying so much of her affection. Yet, still glassy-eyed and absent childish imagination, they sat. Lifeless. Killed by my waning interest. There would be no reviving of that which never possessed life. The warmth of a child's love, kindled within everything, was dying inside me—snuffed by the grip of time's merciless hands.

Deep Calls to Deep

Turmoil rippled. Each neuron aflame. Transient air swirled as the past ushered in the present. I could not go back—I knew it now. Change was upon me. I sat grasping at mental straws. *Where do I go from here? Forward?* Forward seemed so dreadful. Agape at the pending abyss, my mind drew a short, fearful breath. *Maybe this is the valley of the shadow of death.*

Conjured from a bygone voice and dredged from an all-too-neglected pit of church stories, I sat pondering the Twenty-third Psalm. It never made sense. But this felt like death, and the future looked murky. I shivered. Shadows are always cold. *And isn't that where enemies lurk?* I tried again but failed to see my way forward. *Yes*, I answered myself. *The Enemy.*

I sat a long while, captive, in this very present darkness.

But—wait. Wasn't there a Shepherd? The pit of stories had spoken again. I wasn't alone! Different from my party mates, this still small voice came *to* me, not *from* me. It was nice to have a companion. *Yes!* I remembered. *And he was good.*

> *The love I felt and the lessons I learned at that little church said Jesus made all sides right.*

Beside Still Waters

My groping continued. I thought of the teens I knew: cousins, babysitters, sitcom family members, etc. They seemed effervescent. They had a

palpable energy about them, whether planning a sleepover, talking on the phone, or playing sports. With close-to-the-surface bubbling that gurgled at a moment's notice, the girls barely stopped talking, and the boys barely stopped moving.

But in unrestrained emotion, their words and deeds often went unchecked. This impetuous nature overshadowed good judgment, sometimes making them reckless. Because of this, I heard the teen years were rocky, even treacherous and painful. Some don't make it through. I didn't want to stumble on the way to adulthood, ending up scarred and limping through life. I knew enough to know that real danger lay ahead, and I needed to get my footing.

Seeking wisdom, I looked at the past. It was all I knew. Maybe there were lessons to glean for my new journey, something I'd missed or taken for granted that would prove useful.

For one thing, I knew God was always there. From my earliest memories of learning "Jesus Loves Me" at Grandma Toone's knee to my first funeral when Grandpa McVicar died in Boston. I hid in the bathroom that day and cried for a long time. Like a loving father, God heard me and dried my tears.

And I felt his kindness in the people at the little Baptist church on the wrong side of the tracks. That's what we called it. The church sat directly beside our neighborhood, just two blocks from our apartment building. The Illinois Central Railroad lay between. Because we had no car at the time, everywhere we went was measured in foot travel, making this otherwise few-minute jaunt down the street an almost hour-long trek. So, we jumped the tracks to get to church. (Shhh, don't tell anyone!) Maybe it was us on the wrong side of the tracks, but the love I felt and the lessons I learned there said Jesus made all sides right.

Then there was my conscience—a bittersweet thought. It taught me a lot, usually after I did something wrong. Of course, I didn't know it at the time, and that's how it helped me. The trick was to listen. Otherwise, I would have to hear it again later—and louder the next time. It

never let me rest until I paid attention. But once I really listened, I had peace. Funny thing, but it kind of sounded like the still small voice. *Had he always been there too?*

Yes, I saw it clearly now. God and I went farther back than anyone—and he was real. It had been him with me through thick and thin, and it would be him with me going forward. *Maybe that's the only thing I need to know.* Peace settled once again.

☙

The curtain closed on the past as the house lights returned me to my guests. Now relegated to the annuls of time, they sat frozen in this valley-turned-vault to stare in perpetuity. I was thankful for our time together. They played their part well. As for me, the chill was gone. The fantasy world of a child, comprised of everything new and wondrous, had accomplished its purpose in me. Truth had found its footing. Believing was now seeing. My play-turned-plateau dispelled the shadow, growing wide a new vista.

Life Is a Stage

Then it happened. From somewhere deep within came a nudge. Softly at first but persistent. Flight turned to fight as my fledgling teen stirred. I remembered my captor and spit, "It's all *his* fault!" *Him and that dumb apple,* I reasoned. *And the woman.* I dug deeper. "In the real garden the animals did talk!" The gurgling had begun.

Hmmm. The shadow of death . . . You are with me . . . I will fear no evil.[24] It was starting to make sense.

I chuckled as echoes of spring play practice rang in my mind. Inevitably, some extrovert kid would belt out with the gusto of a seasoned thespian, "All the world's a stage!" But I begged to differ. All of life is a stage. Shakespeare was wrong. The real action was playing out in me. One scene—one stage of life—at a time.

---

24. Psalm 23

Lessons Learned in Laughter

by Betty Predmore

S OMETIMES GOD USES a hilarious, often unexpected, moment in our day to teach us a valuable life lesson. The ability to laugh at ourselves is a beautiful gift. Isn't it wonderful that God will use such a gift to help us discern his message to us?

Is More Best?

There's a story in the Bible found in Luke about two sisters, Mary and Martha. Jesus was stopping by to visit them, and Martha was in a flurry. I imagine if I knew that Jesus would be in my home at dinnertime, I might get in a flurry too.

Martha got upset with her sister Mary after Jesus arrived. While Martha worked in the kitchen, Mary sat at the feet of Jesus, listening to his every word. While Martha was caught up in her busyness, Mary was caught up in Jesus.

Like many, I can take on the personality of Martha. I have struggled with being too busy in my adult life. If there is a volunteer position open, I'm your gal. If there is a meeting to get to or a game to watch,

you can find me there. I will raise my hand to volunteer, even when I know I shouldn't.

And we all want to do our civic duty, right? There is always a club or organization to be a part of, which equates to more meetings, often adding more activities to an already overwhelmed schedule.

The ability to laugh at ourselves is a gift. God uses it to help us discern his message to us.

When did we decide that *more* is necessary? Who told us we had to participate in everything to feel valued and important? When did our role as wife and mother become just the steppingstone to all we should be?

I think of Martha and her busy nature. She was so occupied doing the chores and worrying over all that needed to be done that she missed the beauty of sitting at the feet of Jesus. *But the Lord answered her, "Martha, Martha, you are anxious and troubled about many things, but one thing is necessary. Mary has chosen the good portion, which will not be taken away from her"* (Luke 10:41–42 ESV).

Oh, that all of us Martha types could find a way to be more like Mary. There is a balance to be found. What can these two sisters teach us?

What if We Laughed?

On one of those overwhelming afternoons, God spoke to me through hysterical laughter. I was overscheduled with meetings that day, plus my daughter had a volleyball game. Despite all my obligations, she expected me to be there. As a result, I entered rush mode the moment I got out of bed.

There I sat at a ministry board meeting, keeping a close eye on my clock. The game would start soon, and I had to drive to the next town to watch it.

Now, our ministry board was a talkative bunch. We could get sidetracked easily, so the conversation went on beyond the business of the day. I grew more anxious as the meeting progressed. The minutes kept ticking on my clock.

In a last-ditch effort to salvage my schedule, I began to hurry the conversation along. I finally got everyone to wrap up the meeting with just enough time so I could get to my next adventure.

Apprehension set in as I gathered up my papers, grabbed my purse, and got ready to rush out of the building. I could not find my glasses. Believe me, you don't want to be on the highway with me if I'm driving without them.

In a state of panic, with time growing later, I recruited my friends to help me find my glasses. I needed to leave ten minutes ago. I needed their help.

We scoured the room for my glasses. I searched my purse. They looked through their own things just in case my glasses had gotten mixed in. Nothing. No glasses.

By then, I was hysterical. My daughter would be so disappointed if I didn't make it to her game. Even though I knew this, I couldn't leave without my extra set of eyes.

We stood there looking around in confusion. Suddenly one friend erupted in laughter.

A moment later, the other friend joined in.

Me, myself, and I were wondering what in the world was so funny. I saw no humor in knowing I was going to be late for the next appointment on my schedule.

There was a reason no one could locate my glasses. It was a little difficult to find them in my purse, on the table, or mixed in with someone else's belongings when they were, in fact, sitting nicely on my nose right where they belonged.

When I realized that I was wearing them, I took a cue from their abundant laughter and finger-pointing toward my face and joined in the merriment doled out at my expense. It really was funny.

Glasses intact, I headed to the game, having to be okay with being slightly tardy to the volleyball party. I heard the Lord talking to me about my busyness as I drove.

What Does God Want for Us?

God doesn't want us so tied down to our overcommitted schedules that we can't find joy in our lives. There was joy to be found in a ministry board meeting where we could talk and dream about the future and God's plans. Unfortunately, I missed the blessing because of my over-booked calendar. On that occasion, I hurried along, not allowing for time to dream.

There is joy to be found in sitting in the bleachers, cheering on your child. I almost missed those sweet moments.

Even in ministry, we can let ourselves get so busy *doing* that we stop *hearing* what God wants from us. Our busyness can get in the way of our relationship with him. It can also interfere with our home and family ministry, which is our greatest of all.

Where Is Our Value Truly Found?

God really spoke to me that day, during the chaos of rushing around and the hilarity of laughter. He impressed upon my heart the need to slow down, taking time to enjoy this life he has given me. He reminded me that my value is not found in the things I do. I am not defined by the groups I am a member of. My value is not even found in my ministry or the words I write.

Instead, my true value is found in being his beloved daughter, his precious child for which he has beautiful, wonderful plans. Those plans do not include a hectic schedule. It is not his desire for me to feel so overwhelmed that I can't think a meaningful thought or find my glasses that are right on my face.

Let's remember to slow down and soak in. Make time for him. Make time for family. I am resolved to keep my schedule at a pace that I can accomplish without becoming overwhelmed. More white space in our days allows us to look for his lessons.

Don't be afraid to chuckle when a lesson comes through laughter.

Frantic Fuss

by Sandy Lipsky

A LOST OUTFIT ALMOST led to a nervous breakdown. "I can't find my dress!" The voice inside my head shrieked. How could a beloved piece of clothing be treated with such carelessness?

The distance between calm and frantic is not great for me. Anxiety grew in my chest like the expansion of a balloon on the verge of popping. My search for the missing article became more frenzied with each passing minute. Even though guests would soon be en route to my house, I couldn't control a desperate need to continue in the hunt for my mislaid garment.

Prepping for Festivities

Excited to share with neighbors and friends the recent launch of a collaborative devotional, I prepared to host a celebration. I deliberated over each detail for months. Invitees confirmed their plans to attend after receiving the beautiful invitations designed by my niece. I'd even arranged for piano students to provide entertainment.

On the day of the party, food trays retrieved from a local grocery store rested alongside homemade treats. Elaborate outdoor signs placed by a local business announced the book launch party. A clean house stood ready to welcome guests. The neatly stacked books on the dining room table awaited my signature for those wanting to make a purchase. With time to spare, I focused on getting myself dressed and ready.

I needed to prepare an outfit before the event because of my history of clothes anxiety. If I don't lay out my garments or at least plan in my mind what I'll wear the following day, I'm in trouble. Not only does it take four or five attempts to find something acceptable, but my closet floor also becomes a disaster. I've learned stress is avoidable when I map out an outfit the night before.

I chose to replace frantic thoughts with quiet contemplation.

As I lay in bed the night before the bash, I thought of the perfect combination. I pictured myself in my favorite black dress. This cherished knee-length number with its ruffled neck won my heart after I received a beautiful compliment from my husband last year. In my mind, a light gray and cream swirl jacket complemented the sleeveless frock. A contented smile formed. I wanted to look my best as I welcomed guests.

The day of the book launch arrived. Even a rainstorm could not hold back my anticipation. Because of prior planning and preparations, peace walked beside me as I went about my morning routine. I made lunch for my family after readying the food trays for guests. I tidied the kitchen and headed calmly up the stairs to change clothes. First, I arranged my hair in an updo. With my makeup applied, I walked to the closet for my dress and jacket.

Steady hands moved aside garment after garment in search of the chosen slip-on. When I didn't find it in my closet, I scurried downstairs to the laundry room. Back and forth I went—upstairs then downstairs, chasing the notion it must be somewhere in the house. Sweat beaded on my forehead, and a rhythmic pounding began in my chest. I rummaged through items at the back of my closet and pulled out luggage used weeks prior.

How does a responsible, grown woman lose a dress? My favorite dress! With the realization that my outfit had disappeared, I transitioned from a relaxed human to a frantic, deranged creature.

Chaos to Calm

"Breathe Sandy, breathe," I said to myself. Prayer came next. The Lord and I are familiar with my crazy reaction to losing things. It's a generational response passed from parent to child. I now see the "frantic fuss" in my daughter. Amid my internal screaming, I thought of a memorized verse from the Bible. *Be anxious for nothing, but in everything by prayer and supplication, with thanksgiving, let your requests be made known to God; and the peace of God, which surpasses all understanding, will guard your hearts and minds through Christ Jesus* (Philippians 4:6–7 NKJV). As I spoke God's Word, my brain became tranquil. Rational judgment returned. I needed another outfit at once.

The book celebration exceeded expectations.

Then Christmas came and went. I thought about the dress every few days, but the ugly nature of my franticness did not resurface. At least not until another event loomed. "Where is my dress?" I whined. The search began once again. On rare occasions my daughter borrows clothing, but not this time.

I tried to find the same dress online with no result. I chose to replace frantic thoughts with quiet contemplation. When did I last wear it? Nothing came to mind as I sat on the couch with my eyes closed. I decided to be productive and run errands. On my way to the grocery

store, I called my sister and asked her to pray. "God knows where my dress is," I said. We chatted for ten more minutes before ending the call. I knew my sister would intercede on my behalf.

I am not kidding when I say that something amazing happened seconds after our call concluded. As clear as a cloudless sky, I recalled the last time I wore my dress.

Lost and Found

My daughter is a professional violinist. As a family, we had decided to celebrate Thanksgiving near the location of her scheduled performance. She played at an event and then returned to our rented condominium to share in a turkey dinner. My husband and I drove to a neighboring state to attend a funeral the next day while our daughter traveled to another gig. I wore my black dress to the service and then changed in the church's bathroom. The nine-hour drive home required comfortable attire. Could my outfit still be where the funeral took place?

It took me a week to gather enough courage to contact the place of worship in Virginia. When I did, the staff responded at once. After I emailed a description of my missing outfit, an employee sent pictures of what they'd found. A black dress and coverup located in the lost and found closet appeared to be mine. I squealed with joy. The identified items belonged to me. The staff at the church generously shipped the garments within days of discovery—free of charge.

In the seven weeks it took to find my misplaced clothing, I learned a valuable lesson. God cares about each detail of my life. He doesn't want me to fret. Instead, he whispers in my heart, "Come here sweet child. Give your burden to me and go on with your day."

Once I listened to the Lord and released my trouble to him, peace came in the wait, and so did the dress.

Our
Contributors

DENISE MARGARET ACKERMAN'S heart-centered devotions reflect life lessons the Lord is teaching her as she encourages readers to follow him. Denise is a contributing author in the WordGirl's collective *Snapshots of Hope & Heart*. She's been married to her high school sweetheart, James, for forty-eight years. They enjoy creating fun memories with their eight grandchildren on their Upstate New York farm. You can reach her at dackerman.0922@gmail.com or on Facebook.

MINDY CANTRELL resides in Texas with her husband, Bill, and cat-child, Ramjet. Drawing from life experience, she lives out her passion for ministering to ladies' groups and writing devotionals. She plans to publish her current work in progress soon, a Bible study on healing life wounds. Mindy is published in the WordGirls Collective *Snapshots of Hope & Heart* and is an award-winning author in the WordGirls collective *Wit, Whimsy & Wisdom*. Learn more about Mindy at mindycantrell.com.

MARY CURCIO is a retired school educator. Mary's heart is to serve her God, family, and church. An award-winning author, she desires to help women overcome adverse circumstances and leave a God legacy. She has taught Bible studies and Sunday School for over thirty years. Currently, she serves as the women's ministry leader in her church and is Grandma to fourteen grandchildren. You can find Mary on Facebook @mary.o.curcio.

NATASHA LYNN DANIELS is a Christian communicator, author, and the founder of Faithful Hope Ministries. Her purpose is to encourage women to seek joy, live by faith, and hold on to hope. Her words inspire believers to suffer strong for Jesus so they can be filled with the hope and joy of the Lord even when it seems impossible. Natasha's favorite titles are wife and mom. natashalynndaniels.com.

EDNA EARNEY revels in life's diamonds uncovered from coal—our truthful, potential-filled moments in life. She taps into those transformations so her readers see valuable treasures from their own hard days. Together with her husband, Mike, Edna enjoys sharing God's good news for relationships as a Prepare/Enrich marriage mentor and trainer. Retired from teaching English, she has contributed to several compilations, including *Snapshots of Hope & Heart.* Contact Edna on Facebook @TapIntoTransformation.

SALLY FERGUSON usually has to go through the school of hard knocks to learn her lessons. When she lets the Lord use her foibles, it helps others and brings encouragement for those journeying with her through life. Sally lives in Western New York with her husband and dad. She's working on a Bible study for caregivers. Catch up with her at sallyferguson.net.

A retired teacher and administrator, **CAROLYN GASTON** now spends time threading words together and crafting rag rugs. She is an ESL instructor and leads a Bible study for Spanish-speaking ladies. She also facilitates a Bible study for English-speaking ladies through the small group ministry of her church. She loves spending time with family and baking for her ten grandchildren.

NANCY KAY GRACE offers the hope of grace to those she meets. As a cancer survivor, she understands dealing with unexpected challenges. Because life is unedited—certainly not perfect—we need God's grace. She is an engaging Bible teacher, speaker, and award-winning author of *The Grace Impact*. Nancy is married to her favorite pastor. She loves hugs from grandchildren, playing piano, and hiking. Nancy's blog and GraceNotes newsletter signup can be found at nancykaygrace.com.

NANCY GRAVES offers hope, encouragement, and a smile along the way. A storyteller at heart, she shares her life experiences with candor and sincerity, providing personal insight from a biblical perspective. A multi-published author, she has contributed to four women's devotional books, blog posts, and other publications. Nancy can be reached at nleegraves@gmail.com.

Following in the footsteps of Florence Nightingale, **MARY HARKER**, a former nurse, uses the lamp of God's Word to shine light into a dark world. She desires to illuminate the path and guide readers to the truth, freedom, hope, and the power of Jesus. Mary is a contributing author to *Wit, Whimsy & Wisdom, Snapshots of Hope & Heart,* as well as online for christiandevotions.us and The Round Farmhouse.

BECKI JAMES is an ally to all who desire to live in God's presence. With an "old friend" flair, she gently guides hearts to God's throne. Whether ministering with pen or microphone, Becki's way with words nurtures Christ's love to all ages. Encouraging others to live from the inside out, Becki mentors in her community and across the globe. She serves as the TBL Team Chaplain of the Jamestown Jackals in New York. beckijames.com

TERESA JANZEN, MEd, empowers the weary, worried, and wounded to experience God's radical abundance. She is an international speaker, author, coach, and host of the *Radical Abundance* podcast with more than twenty years in leadership and global ministry. Her experience drives her to share inspiring stories with wit and insight, inviting thoughtful dialogue on topics impacting the modern church. Teresa ministers mainly in North America and East Africa.

BETH KIRKPATRICK is a wife, mom, and grandmother who enjoys reading books and laughing with her friends. She strives to be a light for Jesus by being a good listener and sharing encouragement with others. She is a contributing author in the book *Snapshots of Hope & Heart*. After many years of working with elementary students, Beth now works with adults in a literacy ministry, Learning Matters! You can contact her at bethakirk@yahoo.com.

CARIN LeROY and her husband serve with Pioneers, a mission organization that focuses on church planting. She has a passion for others to respond to God in faith by looking for him in every challenging situation. Carin's book *Where No Roads Go* won the Gold Enduring Light Medal for the 2022 Illumination Book Awards. She shares the adventures of living with a tribe and raising their family in the jungle.

LORI LIPSKY'S character-driven stories can transform a reader's perspective. She is the author of *Turquoise Parade* and *Used Cookie Sheets*, both collections of short fiction stories. She and her husband, Mark, live in Sun Prairie, Wisconsin, with a tender-hearted blue heeler. They recently moved to the countryside, where they can relax on their back deck on summer evenings, listen to music, and watch corn grow in the field behind their home. LoriLipsky.com

167

SANDY LIPSKY tries to sit still and compose the things God whispers in her ear. During the day, she writes, teaches piano, and cares for her household. Nighttime finds her reading. Her first published article appeared in *Focus on the Family*, and her newest contributions are in the devotional books *Wit, Whimsy & Wisdom* and *Snapshots of Hope & Heart*. She enjoys Georgia's seasons and spending time with her husband and daughter. sandylipsky.com

CHARLAINE MARTIN helps readers see God's masterful hand in every life adventure. She is a writer, speaker, and contributing author in *Wit, Wisdom & Whimsy* and *Snapshots of Hope & Heart*. She is also a personal trainer and Christian wellness coach. You'll find her and her Boaz putzing around the sky, riding the Florida bike trails, or sharing tickle bugs with their grandkids. You can read her blogs at charlainemartin.com and betotallyfitforlife.com.

DIANA LEAGH MATTHEWS shares God's love through her story from rebel to redeemed. Her day job is as a volunteer coordinator, but at night she writes and hunts genealogy. She gives programs as a speaker, teacher, and vocalist, and also presents historical monologues. Leagh (pronounced Lee) is the author of *History Made Real, Fun with Words, 90 Breath Prayers for the Caregiver,* and others in the Breath Prayers series. She writes the history behind hymns at DianaLeaghMatthews.com.

SUSANNE MOORE empowers women to break free, find healing, and embrace Jesus. She is an abuse recovery coach, speaker, and writer. Susanne is part of the Well Woman Alliance supporting women seeking healing and a contributor on the delightfullyyoursministry.com blog. She is currently writing her memoir. Home is Mansfield, Texas, and you can find her at susanne-moore.com.

Sharing the gospel through writing and speaking is one of **BETTY PREDMORE**'s favorite things to do. She engages audiences with her easy, conversational style. Betty's words inspire women to pause and ponder the possibilities of a beautiful life with Christ. As an author, Christian communicator, and ministry leader, Betty uses every opportunity to encourage women to live their best life in Christ, helping them overcome the strongholds that hold them captive. You can visit Betty at momsenseinc.org.

TERRI ROBINSON is a wife, mother, grandmother, and educator who discovered her love of writing in the third grade. She volunteers at a faith-based recovery home. Terri currently lives in Illinois and enjoys traveling and spending time with her family.

JOANIE SHAWHAN shares true-life stories, offering her reader an eyewitness view of the action. Her Selah Awards finalist book *In Her Shoes: Dancing in the Shadow of Cancer* reflects the value of "Your story plus my story become our stories." An ovarian cancer survivor and registered nurse, Joanie speaks to medical students in the Survivors Teaching Students program. She co-founded an ovarian cancer social group: The Fried Eggs—Sunny-Side Up. Visit Joanie at joanieshawhan.com.

ROBIN STEINWEG finds life is "Sweet in the middle"—like the creamy center of a sandwich cookie! She's a contributing author to the books *Wit, Whimsy & Wisdom* and *Snapshots of Hope & Heart.* Find her writing at *The Christian Pulse, Keys for Kids,* and *Music Teachers Helper* blog. Read her daily prayers for parents at *Prayerenting* on Facebook and encounter bits of positivity with songs on her YouTube channel. Access both at robinsteinweg.com.

Intrigued and inspired by people and personalities, retired school counselor **HALLY WELLS** writes about faith, parenting, and mental illness. Hally's kid sampler pack includes biological, adopted, step, and foster. Each one, along with many students, has awed and exhausted her in beautiful ways. Hally helps overwhelmed parents find practical answers, impactful resources, faith-family support, and divine wisdom—digging deep enough to find the good stuff and reaching high enough to find the best! Visit Hally at hallyjwells.com.

God's Grin Gal, **KATHY CARLTON WILLIS**, writes and speaks with a balance of funny and faith, whimsy and wisdom. She coaches others to remove the training wheels of doubt and not just risk but also take pleasure in the joyride of life. Kathy's been dubbed as WordMama by the WordGirls. Check out her Grin & Grow Break videos on YouTube and her grinning Boston terrier logo in her Grin Gal book series. kathycarltonwillis.com

DAWN WILSON is the founder of Heart Choices Today and blogs at UpgradeWithDawn. com. She is a researcher and reviewer for *Revive Our Hearts* and a regular columnist at Crosswalk.com. She and her husband, Bob, are missionaries living in Southern California. Since being diagnosed with multiple myeloma, Dawn's desire is to encourage women to navigate life's hurts with solid Scripture truth.

Inspired by illuminated manuscripts and stained-glass windows, **LISA-ANNE WOOLDRIDGE** helps others "Live life illuminated." She is often lost in wonder at the beauty of both Creator and creation as she's typing away. Her heartwarming stories have been published in several popular collections. *The Secret Circle*, her first cozy mystery, is now available. You can find her at home—in a land of mountains and valleys that drink in the rain of heaven—or at Lisa-Anne.net.

Acknowledgments

This book was made possible due to some very special people. We want to acknowledge your support and help.

We have grateful gratitudes for:

Our buddy editors. Each essay was edited by at least one buddy editor before the contributing author submitted the piece. Some had input from multiple buddies. We couldn't have done this project without you. In addition to the contributing authors helping each other (a beautiful thing to watch!), we benefited from feedback from Jessica Birdwell, Lisa Thompson, Sharon Burrink, and Judyann Grant. Thank you for helping us out.

Our WordMama, Kathy Carlton Willis. You coordinated the project, mothered us to make improvements, conducted one-on-one and group Zoom sessions to teach ways to make the book better, and edited the complete book. Thank you for caring enough to make sure we give our best.

Our families and friends. You cheered us on and managed without us so we could write. You continue to support our dreams and make us feel as if we're rock stars. You are the book's best team of influencers and launch celebrators! Every time you read and review our work, you help us succeed. *Live & Learn* is possible in part because of you.

Our editor and book designer, Michelle Rayburn. You made sure the book cover design and the interior design reflect our WordGirls brand as well as our hearts. The attention to detail you gave during our edits made sure we followed industry standards. Thank you for our beautiful book!

Our churches. We value the fellowship of faith. Because of our heavenly Father, we are family.

Our Lord. May this book bring you all the glory. It is because of you and your Word that we have words. It isn't always pleasant at the time, but we are grateful for the unexpected classrooms where you teach us life lessons. We are privileged to be your WordGirls.

Our Devotionals

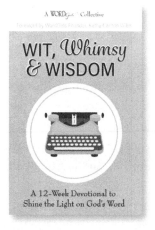

In addition to *Live & Learn*, WordGirls has published two devotionals.

Snapshots of Hope & Heart

When we hear the word snapshots . . . we think moments. In this WordGirls collective, we researched what God's Word says about the topics of hope and heart. *Snapshots of Hope & Heart* includes eighty-four devotions written by thirty-four WordGirls. The authors inserted stories, much like snapshots, to help us capture a true-to-life inspirational insight fitting for the daily Scripture. We hope the takeaways will stick with you throughout the day, similar to the memory of a snapshot long after you've tucked it away.

Enjoy taking a moment with God as you read this devotional. Take your own snapshots as you look through our album of hope and heart.

Our prayer is that these words will deliver word pictures of hope and heart to save to your mind's photo album. In that frame of reference, the Bible is the faith family album deserving to be passed down through the generations.

Wit, Whimsy & Wisdom

Seeking special time with God each day? *Wit, Whimsy & Wisdom* is here to be your guide. In each devotion, look for a concept you can refer back to in your thoughts as you go about your day. The stories will give you some grins, some grace, and some grit to help you through the struggles you face, as well as help you celebrate moments of victory. This three-month devotional is divided into five relevant sections. Feel free to read it straight through or choose what you need that day. Our sections feature Worship & Prayer, Humor, Family, Spiritual Growth, and Women's Issues.

Wit, Whimsy & Wisdom was the first WordGirls devotional, designed to use God's Word and the words of WordGirls to help you fall in love even more with the Word made flesh—Jesus.

Our desire is for you to find nuggets within these pages that make you think, inspire you to worship, and even give you a few laughs along the way.

More 3G Books

Publisher Kathy Carlton Willis has a full line of books. Kathy's boldly practical tips, tools, and takeaways show up in Christian living books, Bible studies, and devo-studies. 3G Books are perfect for small groups or individual reading.

3G Books

The Grin Gal's Guide to Wellbeing: Being Well in Body, Soul & Spirit

Being well begins from the inside out. This book is not just about Kathy's weight-loss and wellness journey. It's a guide for your pursuit of wellbeing. It doesn't provide a program for temporary behavior modification but a process for permanent, God-led change.

On Kathy's quest for improved health, she discovered wellbeing is a balance of body, soul, and spirit. Her coaching style recognizes struggles, victories, aha! moments, and goals. She offers honesty, humor, and occasionally—homework!

The first section has chapters with the following features:

- Heartstrings (Stories)
- Heavenly Insights (Bible Study)
- Help Me! (Tools for Equipping)
- Homework (Making it Real)
- Health Check (Evaluation for Body/Soul/Spirit)
- Hurrahs and Happy Dances (Celebration of Victories)
- Hope Quest (Prayers)

The second section of the book includes practical resources. Join Kathy as a Wellbeing Warrior. Activate personal stewardship by creating your own care plan using the tools of this guide. You won't always see a cure, but you can have a better quality of life.

7 Trials Every Woman Faces: Is Job a Member of My Family Tree? (The Grin Gal's Guide to Trials)

Struggling with life challenges? You are not alone!

Ever wish for a friend who really understood you? *7 Trials Every Woman Faces* offers a virtual friend to lean on. Kathy comes alongside you as she shares insights learned through her own stinky situations.

All life trials fit in the same categories as Job's afflictions (told in the oldest book of the Bible). Whenever Kathy feels as if there's a "kick me" sign on her back, she asks, "Is Job a member of my family tree?" Laughing helps a little.

The chapter segments go along with the family tree theme:

- **Family Album.** Snapshots of heartwarming stories from real life.
- **Family Bible.** Biblical insights to overcome trials from a godly perspective.
- **Family Recipes.** Practical steps to help you grow and succeed God's way.
- **Family Legacy.** Lessons passed along as you help others endure trials.

Learn how to overcome Job-like trials when your family lets you down, friends misunderstand you, your health crumbles, your finances plummet, or others question your faith.

Everyone has trials, but it's the way we deal with hardship that determines not only the outcome but how we cope when we're smack-dab in the middle of them.

The Grin Gal's Guide to Joy: A Story, Study & Steps 7-Week Bible Study

If you've ever felt like the joy, joy, joy, joy down in your heart has gone missing, then this book is for you! Kathy learned that happiness runs and hides, but joy remains when trials show up. Now she's here to share these principles with you in *The Grin Gal's Guide to Joy*.

177

In each chapter:

- **Grin with Joy** tells real-life stories and observations. You'll laugh at Kathy's humorous confessions and wacky insights.
- **Grow with Joy** features a *joy* word study and workbook. Kathy explores what the Bible says and unpacks timely truths.
- **Go with Joy** offers life application. Pick the action steps that help you live a joy-filled life.
- **Give with Joy** equips you to share joy and meet the needs of others. This is when faith becomes ministry.
- Your **Grin with Joy Challenge** describes a joy-challenging scenario to solve.

The Ultimate Speaker's Guide: Practical Tips, Tools & Takeaways

The first book to kick off 3G Books was created with speakers in mind. Packed cover-to-cover with invaluable information, *The Ultimate Speaker's Guide* is the new bible for communicators.

With almost two decades of industry knowledge under her belt, Kathy Carlton Willis has coached hundreds of speakers to help them develop successful speaking businesses. This book covers all the tips, tools, and takeaways you'll need to ensure that your audience increases and your message is heard, including:

- Setting up your business
- Finding a brand that fits
- Getting more bookings
- Polishing your style
- Discovering God's plan for your business

An extensive resource section containing a sample contract, media interviewing tips, fee schedules, checklists, and much more makes *The Ultimate Speaker's Guide* an essential toolkit you'll use time and again.

Made in the USA
Monee, IL
14 August 2022